Scale Up Blueprint

7 Essential Building Blocks for Unstoppable Business, Leadership, and Life

Maja Kazazic

Copyright © 2026 by Maja Kazazic
All rights reserved.

No part of this publication may be reproduced, distributed, or transmitted in any form or by any means, including photocopying, recording, or other electronic or mechanical methods, without the prior written permission of the publisher, except in the case of brief quotations used in reviews, articles, or other non-commercial uses permitted by copyright law.

For permission requests, write to the publisher at:
info@BeaconHousePublishing.com

Published by **Beacon House Publishing**, Palm Harbor, Florida, USA
First edition, **2026**

ISBNs
Hardcover: 979-8-9998390-9-1
Paperback: 979-8-9998390-7-7
eBook (EPUB): 979-8-9998390-8-4

Disclaimer
This book is a work of nonfiction. While every effort has been made to ensure accuracy, the author and publisher make no representations or warranties with respect to the completeness or accuracy of the contents and specifically disclaim any implied warranties of fitness for a particular purpose. The advice and strategies contained herein may not be suitable for every situation. Readers should consult with a qualified professional where appropriate. Neither the author nor the publisher shall be liable for any loss of profit or any other commercial damages.

Trademarks
Scale Up Blueprint™ and related marks are trademarks of Maja Kazazic.

www.MajaKazazic.com

For the builder in you; the part that refuses to stay small.

Table of Contents

Author's Note 1

Introduction 3

Why Some People & Businesses Scale Up And Others Don't 3

Chapter 1: Why Most People and Businesses Get Stuck 11

Chapter 2: The Scale Up Mindset – Thinking Bigger, Acting Smarter 21

Chapter 3: The Scale Up Blueprint™ – The 7 Essential Building Blocks for Unstoppable Growth 34

Chapter 4: Building Block #1 – Support: Leveraging Support & Strategic Networks 49

Chapter 5: Building Block #2 – Mindset: The Power of Mindset & Reframing Challenges 77

Chapter 6: Building Block #3 – Potential: Unlocking Hidden Potential...... 95

Chapter 7: Building Block #4 – Small Steps: The Micro-Actions That Drive Big Growth.. 112

Chapter 8: Building Block #5 – Discipline: The Power of Discipline & Consistency 132

Chapter 9: Building Block #6 - Tenacity: Resilience, Grit & Tenacity in the Scaling Process or Tenacity & Overcoming Setbacks.......... 148

Chapter 10: Building Block #7 – Results: Measuring Results & Sustaining Momentum... 165

Your Legacy 180

The Scale Up Mindset – A Blueprint for Life and Leadership 180

Ready to Go Deeper? 183

Resources 184

Acknowledgments 185

About the Author 186

Index 187

Author's Note

I did not set out to write a book about business alone. I set out to write a book about rebuilding—because rebuilding is what life asked of me, long before it asked me to scale a company. When a single moment split my world in two, I learned that progress is not a straight line. It is a series of choices made in ordinary minutes: stand up, fall down, stand up again.

Years later, inside conference rooms and on factory floors, I watched leadership follow the same pattern. Teams didn't transform because they worked harder; they transformed because they learned what to work on, in what order, together. That is what these Building Blocks are: not tips, not hacks, but a structure you can trust when emotion runs high and time runs short.

If you are reading this in a season of acceleration, I'm happy for you. If you are reading it in a season of starting over, I'm with you. Either way, I hope these pages feel like a steady hand at your back. Use the Blocks. Stack them patiently. Let momentum gather. And when you forget—because you will—come back to the first step you can take from where you are now.

You'll also meet real organizations and public figures in these pages—Elon Musk, Taylor Swift, Jeff Bezos, Martha Stewart, Thomas Edison, Brené Brown, among others. You may admire some and resist others. The goal isn't agreement; it's understanding. I have no affiliations, endorsements, or personal ties to any of them. They're included solely to make the ideas concrete and useful.

SCALE UP BLUEPRINT

If a reference sparks resistance, pause and get curious. Growth asks us to learn from a wide range of sources—even those we wouldn't choose. That openness is how we move beyond our limits.

If you're ready, let's begin.

Maja Kazazic is a Bosnian war survivor turned entrepreneur and keynote speaker. After rebuilding her life in the U.S., she founded an IT company and spent the next two decades helping leaders and teams—from startups to Fortune 100—scale with clarity and momentum. Her Scale Up Blueprint distills those lessons into seven practical Building Blocks that blend resilience, systems thinking, and disciplined execution.

Introduction

Why Some People & Businesses Scale Up And Others Don't

The Art of Scaling Up

Success. For years, I believed success was the destination—the reward for surviving, striving, and pushing through. I thought if I worked hard enough, sacrificed long enough, and endured enough, I'd eventually arrive. And then, life would finally feel complete. I could relax. Coast. I'd know I had made it. I had succeeded.

By my late twenties, I had everything I once believed was impossible—especially for someone with my history. I was living in my dream home near the ocean in Tampa Bay, Florida. I had built a thriving IT company and landed a $150,000/year retainer as my very first client—just three months after launching. I created software that beat out giants like Cigna and Aetna. A little girl from Bosnia, who had survived genocide, built something better than Fortune 100 companies. It felt surreal. I had the freedom, the accolades, the life I once thought only belonged to other people. For most, maybe that would have been enough. But for me? It felt hollow. I couldn't describe it, but when I got to this place of success, but it didn't feel like I thought it would. I expected to be elated—ecstatic even—like fireworks going off in my life and heart. I thought that after the initial excitement, I'd feel happy, relaxed, and content. I'd feel confident about where I was and where I was going. But instead, I felt anxious and at a loss. Hollow and isolated, with a gaping void and no purpose.

Because I was deemed "so successful" while living life somewhat in the public eye, it became even harder to talk about what I was really feeling. I was under pressure to perform, to play the role of the woman who had made it. I didn't feel like I had permission to be vulnerable. I didn't want to come across as ungrateful. Five souls in Bosnia didn't survive the bomb that injured me. They never got these chances. And the very thing that once inspired me—my survival—now made me feel ashamed for wanting more. I was afraid that if I spoke my truth, I'd be seen as ungrateful and, even worse, greedy.

The truth was, I was grateful. Deeply. For how far I'd come. For everything I had. But gratitude alone didn't fill the void. It didn't quiet the deeper questions that kept surfacing in my heart: *Is this why I survived? Was this my purpose? Is this all there is?*

No one tells you that reaching your dreams can be disorienting. That climbing your mountain and standing at the top can come with an eerie silence. That after the adrenaline fades, you might find yourself staring out into the distance wondering… *"Now what?"*

No one prepares you for: **Success is not the end.** Getting to the top doesn't mean you can relax. When you've fought to survive like I have, that truth hits even harder.

I came to this country at sixteen, on the brink of death, with nothing but a rock in my hand, a t-shirt on my back, and a teddy bear I used to bite on and scream into for pain because we didn't have pain medication. I didn't speak a word of English. I endured over 100 surgeries. I had to relearn how to walk. It took 15 years for me to be able to relearn how to run. I finished high school. Graduated college. Built a career. Built a company. All great things.

I wasn't even supposed to be alive. And yet, I had made it. Every box checked. Every milestone reached. Standing on what I thought was the top of my life, at 28 years old....wondering....asking that very same question....***Now what? Is this it?***

But my guilt constantly kept pushing that question away. I kept pacifying myself with answers and distractions that weren't even related. But no matter what life still felt unfinished. Like something was missing.

Until one night, sitting in my living room alone, staring at the stars through my window a question struck my soul like thunder and I dared ask out loud and address head on this elephant in the room:

"Is this all there is? Do I just keep repeating the same day for another 60 years and wait to die? Have I peaked? Is this really what I survived for? I went through all of this to get here, and feel...empty?"

It terrified me. But it was also the most honest moment I'd had in years. I did everything I was supposed to do. I had reached the cultural definition of success, and, by those standards, I was done. Yet, success didn't feel complete, it felt empty. I felt uncomfortable and scared thinking that I had peaked and it was only either downhill or more the same from this point on. Those thoughts didn't sit well with me. I refused to believe that the peak of life feels like this. That accomplishing everything you were supposed to is going to feel like this. It didn't makes sense. Life didn't make sense. And that night I felt this deep knowing that there has to be more to life than "succeeding". Getting to your goals and being done. There had to be something beyond, because if this was it, it would have felt different.

Although the world hadn't told me what to do next, that didn't mean I couldn't go beyond and find out for myself. And after doing deep personal work, I realized something I had never been taught: the goal was never just to succeed. The goal was to *evolve*. To grow. To keep expanding and reaching levels beyond anything I had imagined. That's what we're here for. That's what we're wired for. Not just to survive—but to **Scale Up™.**

To Scale Up™—to dimensions of life and self I didn't even know existed. That's where the real excitement lived. That's where the fulfillment was hiding. In the Art of Scaling Up.

Because if I could survive what I'd survived, what else was possible? If I could scale one impossible mountain, why not another? If I could rebuild myself once, why would I ever stop building?

That night, I made a decision: I would keep scaling. Always. No matter what.

And that single decision changed everything—not just for me, but for every leader, entrepreneur, and organization I would go on to work with.

Why Scaling Up Is the Only Way Forward

That night I realized, success is not the goal. **Growth is.** The moment you stop evolving, you begin to erode. You've seen it happen. So have I. Companies like Blockbuster, Kodak, and Blackberry—once unstoppable giants, now relics of the past. They didn't collapse because they failed. They collapsed because they stopped innovating. They got comfortable. They stood still.

The same thing happens to people. They land the dream job. Build the business. Reach the goal. And then they pause. They stop asking what's next. They stop stretching. They settle. Before long, the very success they worked so hard to build becomes the weight that holds them back.

"The average lifespan of companies on the S&P 500 dropped from about 75 years in 1937 to just 18 years by 2011."

Even giants can become irrelevant without continuous growth. Staying comfortable is the silent threat.

One of the most natural forces in the universe is evolution—constantly expanding toward a better, more refined version of existence. That's why scaling up comes so naturally to all of us. It's why millionaires and billionaires keep making more money. Why successful companies keep getting bigger. Not because they're greedy. Not because they need more to pay the bills. But because once survival is no longer the goal, growth becomes fun. When you're no longer chasing security, you start taking bolder, more meaningful risks. You stop fearing mistakes because you know they won't take you down—they'll teach you. They become data. Insight. Fuel.

And that's when something magical happens. You start pushing boundaries you never thought you could. You begin reaching heights you never even dreamed of. Because people—and businesses—that thrive? They don't stop scaling. They stretch. They grow. They lead. They change the world. Which is why the only way forward... is to keep scaling up.

Why Working Harder Isn't the Answer

When it comes to scaling up, most people think the answer is to work harder. More hours. More hustle. More grind. But scaling isn't just about effort—it's about **elevation**.

It's about aligning your **mindset**, your **strategy**, your **environment**, and your **support** system so that growth becomes your default setting. Because real growth doesn't come from trying harder. It comes from building smarter.

Scaling isn't a personality trait. It's a process. A repeatable system. A way of thinking, operating, and evolving. It's about creating a culture—within yourself or your organization—where evolution is expected. Where momentum is the norm. Where breakthroughs are inevitable. It's about rising to the next level of existence, where scaling up becomes as natural as breathing—and the only way forward.

The Scale Up Blueprint™: Your Roadmap to Exponential Growth

After decades of navigating my own journey—first to survive, then to thrive—I became obsessed with understanding what separated those who broke through from those who stayed stuck. I studied world-class leaders, high-performing teams, fast-scaling companies, and individuals who defied the odds. What I discovered was both surprising and empowering: they all had a piece of the formula. Some focused on discipline. Others emphasized mindset. Some leaned into vision, strategy, or support. They mostly focused on the parts that they were lacking, their weak point, completely ignoring and taking for granted necessary building blocks that they already possessed.

Take Simon Sinek's iconic concept: "Start With Why." It's brilliant. It's accurate. And for many companies, it works, especially for those that already have other foundational elements in place. But here's what often gets missed: companies that already have a strong purpose may still struggle if they lack support systems, structure, or discipline. Leaders who succeed using Sinek's framework tend to assume it's the strategy without realizing it only works so well because the other pieces were already in place.

Now look at Mel Robbins' "5 Second Rule." It's a game-changer for those who need help building discipline. But for organizations that already operate with structure and are lacking clarity, purpose, or strategy? It doesn't move the needle in the same way.

These aren't failures of the strategies. They're gaps in the system.

That's when I realized: no one has the full structure. Each popular method was offering a piece of the puzzle. But what about the whole picture? What's the formula that works regardless of where you're starting, or what you're missing?

That's how the 7 Building Blocks were born.

After years of research, reflection, and real-world implementation, I discovered that sustainable success is built on **seven essential building blocks**. Even more important, they have to be stacked in a specific order. Each building block is a foundation for the next. Miss one, and the whole system starts to wobble. But when all seven are aligned and strong scaling becomes inevitable. That's what this book is about.

The **Scale Up Blueprint™** is a framework designed to unlock unstoppable growth. It's the structure behind lasting transformation—whether you're building a business, leading a team, or scaling your life. And it works. Whether you're just starting out or you've already hit a plateau and want to reach new heights. Inside, you'll learn how to identify and strengthen each building block. How to shift from hustle to high-leverage strategy. How to escape the plateau trap and generate momentum that builds on itself. This isn't theory. It's a proven system. It's your roadmap.

This Is Your Moment

The fact that you're here means something. You're not reading this by accident. It means you're done settling for "good enough." It means you're ready to reach higher—for your life, your organization, your mission, your future. And that's where growth begins. The moment you realize you want that next level. I am proof that scaling up isn't reserved for the lucky or the chosen. It's available to anyone bold enough to ask: **"What if there's more?"** For you, your family, your organization, your life.

So take a breath. You're not starting from scratch. **You're starting from strength.** And I will show you the way. The next level is already within reach. Let's Scale Up™. Together.

Chapter 1

Why Most People and Businesses Get Stuck

Why Success Is the Enemy of Growth

When we talk about what holds people back, most assume it's failure—the wrong decision, a missed opportunity, the dream that never quite got off the ground. But in reality, what traps most people—and most businesses—isn't failure. It's *success*. Although it sounds counterintuitive, success can be one of the greatest traps of all—because it feels safe. It feels comfortable. It feels like an end. It convinces you that you've arrived, that the hard part is over, that you can finally stop pushing.

And that's exactly when growth stops.

Think about it. How many businesses dominated their industry—until they didn't? How many professionals climbed to the peak of their careers—only to plateau for years? How many leaders built something extraordinary, only to watch it fade—slowly, quietly—without even realizing when the decline began? It happens everywhere. And far too often. Not because people aren't talented. Not because they aren't hardworking. Not because they aren't ambitious. But because **comfort is the silent killer of growth**. Success creates a false sense of security. It tricks you into thinking you've "made it"—that the hard part is over and now you get to ease off the gas. But that's the moment momentum dies. And what's worse, most people don't even realize it's happening until it's too late.

The Hidden Barriers That Keep People and Businesses Stuck

The reason people and companies fail to scale is something deeper than lack of talent, intelligence, or drive. Often, the same people who built the company are there to witness its downfall. Not because they got worse, but because they stopped evolving. Why? The reason is something deeper. Much more subtle. It's the *hidden barriers* that quietly creep in the moment success makes us feel safe.

Let's go through each of these barriers to get familiar so you can start recognizing them. After this we will go over the entire ScaleUp™ Blueprint. This way you will be equipped to recognize signs of stagnation and the barriers that are keeping you from scaling up.

Barrier One: The Plateau Trap

This is the danger of "good enough."

It happens when you hit a milestone, achieve a goal, or reach a level of success you once thought was impossible. You convince yourself it's time to coast. You stop innovating. You stop challenging yourself. You stop asking what's next. Unfortunately, growth doesn't happen on autopilot.

The movie rental company Blockbuster is the perfect example of a killer plateau. At their peak, they had over 9,000 stores across the country and total market dominance. Netflix was just a blip on the radar, with their mail-in DVDs. Some of you reading this book won't even have a clue of what I am talking about. At that time, Blockbuster was the king, and Netflix was a new emerging company. Why worry about some startup?

We know how that story ended. But that's the trap. Blockbuster believed their position was permanent. They ignored the shift to digital. They stopped evolving. They coasted on what had worked in the past, trusting that it would continue to work in the future. As the world moved forward, they stayed still. There is no such thing as staying as you are. Because this lesson is simple: **if you're not actively scaling, you're silently slipping,** whether you realize it or not.

> *"Research from Harvard Business Review shows that companies that focus solely on maintaining the status quo after reaching success are more likely to underperform within five years."*
>
> *(Source: HBR, "The Perils of Success")*

Barrier Two: The Perfection Paradox

Perfection is one of the most dangerous traps of all. It convinces you to wait—wait until the plan is perfect, until the timing is ideal, until every detail is figured out. But waiting kills momentum. If you look at some of the most successful companies in the world, they launch products before they're perfect. In a digital world, this is now more obvious than it used to be with brick-and-mortar companies. Take Apple, for example. They release the first version as soon as it's good enough—and refine it later. Updates come. Improvements follow. Progress is constant. They don't wait for perfection. Instead, they build excellence through action. You must do the same. Whatever it is that you're trying to scale up, start working on it. Get it out there. Keep refining as you go. That's how you build momentum—and momentum is what propels you to the next level.

"A study by the University of Scranton found that over 90% of people who wait for 'perfect timing' never follow through with their goals."

(Source: University of Scranton Goal Study)

Barrier Three: The Fear Factor

Fear is the third, and perhaps most paralyzing, barrier. We face fear in all aspects of our lives. But in corporations and the financial world, fear is amplified—because loss often means destruction. The destruction of people's lives (if you're running an organization), or the loss of a home, income, or security. It's not easy to manage this fear. Beyond the fear of financial collapse, there are quieter fears that stop us from scaling up, like fear of failure. Fear of judgment. Fear of losing what you've worked so hard to build. So people play it safe. They protect the status quo instead of pursuing the next level.

There are countless personal and professional development tools out there, each offering different strategies to help you reach your goals—but all of them agree on one truth: **growth doesn't live in the comfort zone.** If you want to grow, you must be uncomfortable. You must learn to manage your fear. You must learn how to make fear your ally, not your enemy. Because, believe me, even fear has its purpose. Fear teaches us calculated risk taking, which is necessary part of business and life if you want to grow. You must master how to take calculated risks while managing the discomfort that comes with them.

Take Amazon, for example. It started as an online bookstore. Jeff Bezos chose that model because, after reviewing different markets, it posed the lowest initial risk with the greatest potential to scale. (A calculated risk.) But he didn't stop there. He kept expanding—until Amazon became something that changed the world and the way we shop. Each time the business expanded, he was forced to face new fears and taking new calculated risks. Imagine if Bezos had been too afraid to try. If he'd been unwilling to risk the unknown, we wouldn't be talking about one of the most innovative companies in modern history—one that impacted thousands of brick-and-mortar stores and reshaped global commerce. **Playing not to lose is the fastest way to lose everything.**

"Neuroscience research shows that our brain processes fear in the same region that governs logic and decision-making, meaning unmanaged fear can cloud sound business judgment."

(Source: Harvard Center on the Developing Child)

Breaking Through

To scale up, you have to get familiar with breakthroughs.

All breakthroughs come from pushing boundaries, believing when no one else does, and continuing to move forward no matter how long it takes. Breakthroughs are powerful tools. They can, and do, catapult us into an entirely new world. I know the power of breaking through because I've lived it.

For years after my injury, everyone told me to settle. The doctors, the specialists, the well-meaning voices all said the same thing: *"Be grateful you survived. Be happy that you're walking. Let go of the dreams you once had."*

SCALE UP BLUEPRINT

Running? Playing sports? Living without limits?
Impossible now. For awhile, I believed them. When enough people tell you to shrink your dreams, you start to wonder if they're right. But deep down, there was a quiet, persistent part of me that refused to give in. I hadn't survived war, escaped death, and rebuilt my life from nothing just to live a smaller, more limited version of it. So I kept searching. Because surviving wasn't enough. I wanted to *run*.

Fifteen years of dead ends. Fifteen years of hearing, *"No, I'm sorry—your injuries are just too different, too complex. There's nothing we can do."* Fifteen years of traveling the country, visiting every prosthetic company I could find, trying every piece of technology, every possible solution, only to keep hitting walls that felt unbreakable. But I couldn't stop. Because settling would've been its own kind of death. The slow kind. The conscious kind. Physical death is something you aren't aware of. But this? This was something I would have to witness every day. I couldn't bear the thought of dying that way—fully alive, yet cut off from the life I knew was possible. To live, I knew I had to run. I had to be free. I had to live fully, without limitation.

Then, on a day that seemed like any other, in a place I never expected, everything shifted. I was standing in front of a large dolphin tank, watching trainers work with a dolphin named Winter. She had lost her tail, the very thing that gave her freedom, in a crab trap. I sat on the bench, leaning in for a closer look. Something about her story echoed mine. Was this a different kind of death for a dolphin? Was she trapped the way I was? Floating, yet unable to truly swim? There she floated, still, quiet, staring back at me.

Then, a trainer walked up to the edge of the tank, slid a prosthetic tail onto her body... and just like that Winter started to swim. I was shocked. I couldn't quite believe what I was seeing. In that moment, something in me broke wide open. I had a thought that would change everything:

"This dolphin has injuries that are different. Whoever made her tail—maybe they could make my leg? If they found a way for a dolphin to swim again... maybe they could help me run."

I didn't know who "they" were. But one thing I knew: these were people who refused to settle. They were pushing boundaries. They were scaling. They were my kind of people. And for the first time in years, I let myself fully believe again. Maybe "impossible" wasn't the end of the story. Maybe it was the beginning.

To make Winter swim, they had to create a special prosthetic tail, which was really the easy part. Dolphins have extremely sensitive skin, so they needed to be able to fit the tail to her without hurting her skin. The conventional methods didn't work so they created something brand new. A revolutionary gel. This gel made the impossible possible. I contacted the same team who helped Winter and shared my story. Willing to keep pushing limits, they offered to try the same gel and technology to fit me with a new prosthetic. I was one of the first people to use Winter's Gel on a human. It was remarkable. Today, this gel is used by amputees all over the world—especially war survivors like me or US Veterans, whose injuries are complex, nerve-sensitive, and often deemed unsolvable. That gel, created for a dolphin's fragile skin, turned out to be exactly what we needed.

Equipped with Winter's Gel and training from a Paralympic athlete, I ran. For the first time in fifteen years. The wind hit my face. My heart pounded—not from fear, but from freedom. And for the first time in so long, I felt wildly, fully alive. Two weeks later, I was playing tennis, pain-free.

Three months later, I crossed the finish line of my first 5K. After reaching those goals, after celebrating those wins, I realized something that changed me forever:

Every limit I thought was permanent... wasn't.
Every barrier I thought was unbreakable... wasn't.
Every voice that told me to settle... was wrong.

But the most dangerous voice wasn't theirs. It was mine. Without realizing it, I had started to believe that "good enough" was all there could be. That my current success was fine. That it would have to do. Until Winter. Until that breakthrough. I realized that the same walls that hold us back in our personal lives are the ones that hold back businesses, leaders, and organizations. The patterns are the same. The resistance is the same. The fear is the same. So are the breakthroughs. The difference between those who stay stuck and those who scale isn't luck. It isn't timing. It isn't talent. It's the decision to keep going. To keep searching. To keep pushing boundaries and keep believing there's a way forward—even when no one else sees it. Growth doesn't happen by avoiding resistance. It happens when we use resistance as fuel. On the other side of every "impossible" is the life, the business, and the impact you were meant to build. The only way out... is through. Just like Winter's Gel changed the world, you never know how you—and your growth—might do the same.

The Shift That Unlocks Scale

Scaling isn't just about strategy. It's about mindset. In fact, nothing works if your mindset isn't set for success. If you want to unlock your next level, you have to start thinking bigger. You have to ask yourself:

Am I playing not to lose—or am I playing to win?
Am I protecting what I've built—or am I expanding it?

Growth mindset requires risk. It requires discomfort. It requires a relentless commitment to what's possible. But most of all, it requires the awareness to recognize the barriers—and the courage to break through them. Because, **if you're not actively growing, you're already shrinking.** Recognizing the forces holding you back is the first step, but breaking through requires more than awareness. It requires a system and a blueprint, which is exactly what you'll find in this book. So take a breath. Look at where you are now. Look at where you want to be. And get ready. Once you learn how to break through these barriers, you won't just succeed. **You'll Scale Up™.**

Shareable Content:

Your Turn:

What's your Winter moment? Where in your life or business have you started to settle—and where are you ready to scale?

Share your breakthrough—or what's been holding you back—using #ScaleUpBlueprint on social media. Let this be the moment you say: Enough. I'm ready to scale.

Social Media Ready:

"Success is not a finish line. It's a trap disguised as safety." #ScaleUpBlueprint

"The moment you stop growing isn't when things fall apart. It's when they start fading—and you don't even notice." #ScaleUpBlueprint

"Comfort is the silent killer of greatness." #ScaleUpBlueprint

"If you're not breaking through, you're building a cage." #ScaleUpBlueprint

Chapter 2

The Scale Up Mindset – Thinking Bigger, Acting Smarter

Your next level requires your next level mindset. Some people hit a certain level of success and stay there forever. Others keep expanding, evolving, and scaling beyond what anyone expected. They seem to break through every barrier that holds others back. What's the difference? It's not intelligence. It's not talent. It's not even luck. **It's mindset.** If you want to scale up—truly scale, not just succeed once—the first thing that has to expand is your thinking.

Most people set reasonable goals. Goals that fit within reach. Practical. Smart. Safe. Before my injury, I did the same thing. We're all taught to do that. Figure out where we are, secure our spot, and then gently rise, little by little. But life shoved me in a direction where that wasn't an option. It shoved me so far down that what most people consider basic were, for me, unimaginable pipe dreams. A home. A family. Going to school. Speaking the language. Driving a car. Walking. Running. These things weren't luxuries for me, or even a given - they were impossibilities. While others worked toward better cars or bigger houses, I was fighting for my life. And after that, surgery after surgery - so many of them that I stopped counting after 100. Running? A house by the beach? Starting a company? That wasn't a dream. That was science fiction.

I had many people tell me I'd never do any of it. The only reason I didn't listen is because I couldn't imagine my life without those things. Living a disabled existence, a shadow of a life, grateful for crumbs? That wasn't an option. I believed I was worthy of more, therefore I will have it. Maybe it would take me longer to get there. Maybe it would be harder. But that didn't matter. I was clear and I knew what I wanted, I knew what I was worthy of, and I went after it.

Like a symphony unfolding in perfect rhythm, I kept achieving one statistically improbable goal after another. At the time, I didn't overthink the how. I just kept moving forward, making decisions, and watching the progress unfold. I wasn't worried about outcomes or how I would get there. I just knew they would happen. The alternative never crossed my mind. But something strange happened as I got more and more goals completed (and once I became more integrated into Western society). Even though the goals were statistically easier to achieve, and I was the master of scaling up, I felt different. They felt harder to reach, risker and scarier. I could't understand why until I spent some time analyzing the details.

One of those "scary goals" I set for myself was to make $10,000,000. I remember how scared I was to even think it, let alone say it out loud. It took me years to bring myself up to even set it as a goal, let alone go after it. I remember wondering: How would I do it? What does that even mean? What does it look like to have $10,000,000? I had more questions than answers. That made me pause. Why? Why, all of a sudden, was I questioning my ability to do something? Was it because I wasn't capable? Was it too big of a leap? What was really going on? I had to go back and ask myself: why had some of the more impossible goals in my past come so easily, without fear, while more recent goals, which were statistically more probable, felt so out of reach?

Think about this number: $10,000,000 For some people reading this book, that number will be too large. They can't even conceptualize it. For others, that number may seem reasonable and easy to get. And for some, that number may be laughable because they are used to working in billions. This is exactly the same number, same goal - but it feels different depending how you look at it. Which made me realize - it's not about the number or the goal. It was all about my mind and the mindset I was carrying with me. Let me show you what I mean.

After I was severely injured, I was brought to a makeshift hospital. My injuries were extensive, and my leg was amputated without anesthesia. The only way to fight the infection in my body was to cut away infected flesh daily. There were no antibiotics. No painkillers. No real medicine at all. We were 60,000 civilians surrounded by two armies, constantly bombed and cut off from food, water, electricity, or any outside contact. There was no way in or out.

I laid in that bed 24/7, hovering on the edge of death, and I didn't even realize it. In fact, I was so positive that the room I stayed in became known as "The Happy Room," because I laughed and joked all the time. I was just a 16-year-old kid who loved life and cared about sports. I didn't think about the war, how wounds healed, or how badly I was injured. The only thing I knew was that I would be okay. One day, I would run again. Play sports again. I didn't know how or when, and I didn't care about the details. I just *knew*. In fact, I talked about it constantly, as if I'd be running again by next week.

One day, an injured man who was laying in the bed across from mine and had a full view of my injuries daily, just snapped. He was apparently sick of hearing me talk about running and my relentless optimism. Out of nowhere he started yelling at me: *"Shut up! Shut up! What do you mean you're going to be running? You're crazy! There is no way you'll be running. I can take a f*ing grapefruit and shove it down your heel. You'll be lucky if you live, let alone walk, and you will never run."*

I was in shock. First of all, no one had ever yelled at me like that. But to yell at me for being optimistic? That took a different kind of cruelty. I didn't know what to say or how to react. I was speechless. But despite the shock, one question echoed in my head: Is he right?

Up until that point, I had never looked at my injuries. I knew they were bad, but I had purposely avoided facing the full extent of them. Now, I could no longer ignore it. So I asked for a mirror. I removed the bandages so I could see every injury - one by one - and face the reality of what was actually happening.

I started with my left arm. It was the least impacted, but I could still see thousands of tiny shrapnel fragments peppered in my skin. *So much metal*, I thought. It didn't hurt much, but it looked strange. Then I looked at my amputated leg, it was like something from a cartoon, not at all what I expected. It stunned me to see how much healing would have to happen for this wound to close.

I moved my attention to my other leg. A couple of larger pieces of shrapnel were lodged half in, half out, on my thigh, waiting for my body to expel them. Then, as I looked below my knee, I saw that my leg was shredded like I was in a Fruit Ninja game gone wrong. Five or six inches of tibia and fibula were completely exposed and shattered. I thought, *Wow, this will take some time to heal. It's pretty bad.*

And finally, I turned the mirror toward my ankle and heel. My heart pounded. I could barely twist into the correct position to see it, but when I did, I understood exactly what that man meant. He was right. You really could shove a grapefruit down my heel. There was a deep, gaping hole, so wide and hollow that you could see the heel bone itself. I was devastated. I got sick to my stomach and felt physically ill. I couldn't believe what I was seeing. It was really bad. So much worse than I even considered.

Now I had a choice. Do I acquiesce to this man's reality, the one where I should feel lucky just to be alive? Or do I stay in my own bubble, where I believed I would walk and run again soon?

It was simple logic that actually saved me. I thought to myself: *Yes, this IS in fact really bad.* I might die. If from nothing else other than infection or lack of blood. I am already seeing everything with a yellow tint, and I am kind of tired all the time. Maybe I am dying already. But there is nothing I can do about that - what's going to happen is going to happen. I can't control that part. If I'm going to die tomorrow or next week, I'll die either way, regardless of what I am thinking, regardless if I'm miserable or happy. The only choice I have really is if I want to die happy or miserable. So why not choose joy? Why not believe in something better?

There was absolutely no benefit to giving up or thinking horrible thoughts. Or worrying. None of that would save me. It would only bring me down. If these were my final days, I didn't want to waste them in fear or despair. So I made a decision to think and feel I was going to be happy and running soon. Die or not. I handed the mirror back and proclaimed to myself: *F*** you and your negativity. I'll live happy. If I am going to die, I will die happy, with thoughts and feelings of me running free.*

And from that point forward, I embraced happiness in every situation. No matter what life gave me, I looked for a way to find joy. I chose belief over doubt. I chose it again. And again. And again.

What I didn't realize at that time is that by making that decision, I had set up my mindset for success for life. I had unknowingly created a Scale Up Mindset—the kind of mindset that would keep helping me break through and rise, no matter what life threw at me. Almost immediately something fascinating happened. Once I made the decision to live as though I'd survive, walk, and run—things started to shift. Just a couple weeks later, a woman named Sally Becker showed up at my bedside with an interpreter. She was a civilian artist from London who somehow secured permission from the enemy army to enter our side of town and rescue three injured children. I was one of the candidates, if I wanted to go. I had to decide quick because she was leaving in twenty minutes.

Twenty minutes later, I was being carried on a stretcher out of the war zone with a total stranger, not knowing where I was going or what would happen next. But I wasn't scared. I just knew it would be okay. It is this mindset that shifts the universe in your favor. It's not logic. It's not your plans or your control, trying to check off items off of a list to "make it happen." It's the deep knowing and believing in the future you want to have that you feel worthy you deserve.

We hear a lot today about manifestation, as though it's a new concept. But manifesting is simply the way nature works. It's what I call our **Inner Sonar**—the internal signal that communicates to the ether what it is we want, deserve, and need. The universe makes it happen. These aren't the words you speak or your conscious thoughts. This is your being speaking out to the universe your deepest desires, thoughts, feelings, and beliefs. The ones you may not be even aware of.

As abstract as this might sound, it's backed by science. A study published in Psychological Science found that people who strongly believe in manifestation report higher aspirations, greater optimism, and a stronger belief in future success—even before any action is taken. Another long-term study from the University of Florida tracked individuals over decades and found that those with higher core self-belief—meaning they trusted in their own competence—earned more over time. Why? Because they pursued better opportunities and believed they could achieve more, so they did.

Also, Google, Microsoft, and LinkedIn have all integrated mindset training, visualization, and "prime-the-brain" techniques into their leadership development programs. These companies recognize that scaling innovation and results begins with internal belief systems and neuroplasticity-based tools.

Even in business, this is reflected in numbers: in a study of insurance salespeople, those who believed they'd succeed, sold 35% more than their less optimistic peers. Their belief created their results. That's co-creation. That's Inner Sonar in action.

There was absolutely no way I could have logically planned, controlled, or prepared for what it took in order for me to survive and eventually live a "normal" life. I couldn't have planned or checked off 100+ surgeries. I couldn't have planned on being evacuated to Germany, then the U.S.A. for medical treatment, by an artist from London. Nor even imagine meeting Winter the dolphin whose prosthetic tale would be the key to my life, or then training with a Paralympic athlete. These things were completely unthinkable to me. If I am being honest, I didn't even know some existed. They were about as possible and probable as me going to space now. But they did happen, and I am convinced my mindset got me there.

Beyond blindly believing and trusting the outcome, another important point worth noting is that through out this process I felt I was worthy of a normal life. I was worthy of living. Of walking. Running. Going to school. I felt like those things weren't too much to ask for, and that I truly deserved them. This is a necessary part of achieving your goals - believing that you are worthy of them.

"Your mindset is your signal. What you believe, you begin to build—even before the world catches up."

Last but not least, I was easily able to imagine this normal life for myself. Why? Because I had lived that life before. I already knew what having a home felt like, what walking and running felt like, what it was like to go to school. All of these were familiar feelings I could slide into. I could close my eyes and relive those memories. Those memories made it real, reachable, and made it my reality. It's a widely known fact now that our brain doesn't distinguish between what's real and what's imagined. Imagining myself running and walking was a clear way to keep getting better and move towards my goals.

Before we move to breaking my two goals down, let's pull out the three most important parts of the Scale Up mindset:

1. **Feeling worthy of the outcome, and believing you deserve it. (Feeling it deep down, not just saying it.)**

2. **Trusting the outcome, without knowing or being concerned about the details. (Who, how, what, where, when - simply trusting that it will happen.)**

3. **Knowing what having that outcome feels like to you. (Being able to close your eyes and imagine you already got it. Being able to feel it.)**

Now the we know these three things let's compare the two goals:

Goal 1: Coming back from a brink of death to run a 5K marathon, after such a severe injury, while stuck in a makeshift hospital surrounded by two armies, **versus**

Goal 2: Making ten million dollars working from my paid-off house five minutes from the beach in Florida while running a successful business since 2004.

It's pretty clear that the second is easier to do. In fact, some would say that making $10,000,000 is a natural next step in a life of an entrepreneur in the USA. Also, the steps and leaps required to earn money in the USA are far less and much easier than building a brand new life after a genocide, from the ashes. If I were making bets I'd put my money on the second goal.

But in my mind and heart, that goal was far more difficult to achieve, despite it actually being easier, more fun, and more likely. Not to mention - that second goal had no pressure. If I don't make $10,000,000, nothing will happen. Who cares. I already live a full and happy life and have everything I need. By all counts, Goal 2 should really be a fun breeze. But it wasn't — it was scary, and huge, and impossible. When I asked myself why, I found my answer in the 3 criteria I mentioned above.

At the beginning, as I was reaching my goals smoothly, I met these three criteria easily—I felt worthy of living a normal life and, as a result of feeling worthy, I believed it would happen. And because I believed it deep down, I radiated that life. Because I had lived that life before, it was so easy to imagine myself doing all of it. I met those 3 criteria with ease, and so the goals, no matter how impossible or improbable, came with ease.

But as we move forward to more recent goals, like making $10,000,000, then my mindsets started to waver. I started questioning my worthiness. I grew up in a small country where wealth was measured in people, not dollars, and the concept of having "huge" amounts of money was strange and look down on. This was before the war.

After the war, my entire family and country have been devastated; having too much money is actually seen as showing off—embarrassing in some way. Strangely enough, too little money is seen that way too. I come from a culture that has this acceptable middle ground where you're supposed to exist. Too much (whatever that is) or too little (whatever that is) is seen as "wrong." Within me, I carried this belief that I shouldn't and couldn't have more. That life belonged to "other," people that were born lucky, more worthy than I was. And I didn't belong there.

Because I didn't feel like I was worthy, believing and trusting that I could get it came into question. I couldn't just let go and let universe do its thing because I didn't believe deep inside. So I did what we all try to do when we feel like this - I started to "plan" and control the outcome—which is what we do when we don't simply trust. This kind of planning is not only hard, it's impossible. The universe will always have better and quicker solutions than you ever will. Your job is to work on your mindset so you can co-create your future. Not to try and control the world into something you are talking yourself into to begin with.

To make matters worse, I had not only never lived as a millionaire, I didn't even know any millionaires. I had no idea what it meant to be a multi-millionaire. This was reserved for people in the movies, not real life. I couldn't even imagine what that life was like. What does it look like to have ten millions of dollars in a bank account? What does that feel like? I had no idea.

The lack of the 3 criteria made scaling up to the next level a lot more difficult. This is why there is no blueprint, no formula, no book that can help you reach your goals until your mindset is aligned. Until you have a winning, Scale Up Mindset and until you believe the what you are after is truly possible and you are worthy of it. Until you act like its already yours. Not just say it, but believe it in your core the way I believed I would run. This is why the biggest limitation to scaling isn't your competition, your timing, or your circumstances—it's your thinking.

If you bring a small mindset into a big opportunity, you will always shrink the opportunity to match your mindset. If you bring a **Scale Up™ mindset**, you'll expand into something bigger than you ever imagined. Let's explore these a bit further.

Once I realized that thinking small keeps you small and was able to outline the three mindset shifts I mentioned above, I was able to adjust and scale up. That is when I made a firm decision that I would make $10 million. Not someday. Not "maybe." Not "if everything goes right." I declared it. Boldly, audaciously, and with zero clue how I was going to get there. That was the thing: I didn't need to know how.

The number itself didn't matter. It could've been five million, twenty million, or more. What mattered was the *shift*. I wasn't just changing my goal, I was changing my identity. I started thinking like someone who builds empires, not someone who inches forward. I stopped asking, "What's realistic?" and started asking, "What's possible?" "What do I *want*?" That shift changed everything.

Just like clockwork, the universe delivered. I began to notice opportunities I had never seen before. I made decisions from a place of purpose and power, not fear or hesitation. I started scaling up mentally long before the external results showed up. That's what separates those who plateau from those who rise.

Your business, your career, and your life will never outgrow your mindset. Scaling doesn't start with strategy. It starts with belief. It starts by thinking like a leader, even when you don't yet feel like one. It starts by making bold decisions, even when the outcome is uncertain. It starts by imagining a future that's bigger than your past, and acting like it's already yours. So ask yourself right now:

Are you setting goals that stretch you?

Are you taking risks that reflect the level you want to play at?

Are you thinking like someone who's already scaling?

If not, now is the moment to change that. Before we build anything in the physical world, we build it in our minds first.

"The universe doesn't respond to your plans. It responds to your belief."

In the next chapter, we'll lay out the full **Scale Up™ Blueprint** and the 7 essential Building Blocks that create unstoppable momentum in your business, your leadership, and your life. You'll see how they fit together, why the order matters, and how to start applying them right now.

Let's keep going. You're just getting started.

Shareable Content:

Your Turn:

Quick Win

1. Write down one bold, outrageous goal that excites and scares you.
2. Underneath it, write how you'd feel if it were already true.
3. Then ask yourself: Do I believe I deserve this? Am I trusting it will happen?
4. If not—that's where the real work begins.

Share your mindset shift or bold goal using #ScaleUpBlueprint and tag me. I want to see how you're stretching into your next level—and celebrate with you.

Social Media Ready:

"Your next level doesn't start with strategy. It starts with belief."
#ScaleUpMindset #LeadershipGrowth

"If you bring a small mindset into a big opportunity, you'll shrink it to match. Scale your mind first."
#ScaleUpBlueprint #ThinkBigger

"Manifestation isn't magic—it's focus. It's a signal to the world that you're ready to receive more."
#InnerSonar #ScalingUp

"The hardest goals aren't always the most improbable—they're the ones we believe we don't deserve."
#SelfWorth #NextLevelYou #ScaleUp

Chapter 3

The Scale Up Blueprint™ – The 7 Essential Building Blocks for Unstoppable Growth

Success isn't random, it's built. For years, people have asked me how I did it. How I went from having nothing - no money, no connections, no roadmap - to building a thriving company, winning awards, and creating a life that once felt impossible. That question is what led me to explore the "success formula." I wanted to understand how and why some people scale up from insurmountable odds, while others keep spinning in the same circle.

I must admit, this question always stunned me. It felt like the person asking expected a dramatic, cinematic answer. But the truth is far simpler, and far more powerful. I didn't just wake up one day and figure it all out. I didn't have some secret that others didn't. What I had was an obsession with understanding what works. That obsession started because I literally had to survive, and then it grew from there. I became a student of success. I studied my own wins and my own failures. I paid attention to what moved me forward and what held me back. I watched leaders, teams, companies, and high performers across every industry. I listened, learned, tested, failed, and refined. Over time, something emerged. I saw patterns that repeated. Foundational elements that showed up over and over again. Not just in my life, but in every story of growth I encountered. These elements weren't magic. They weren't mystery. They were building blocks. Once I saw them, I couldn't unsee them.

It became obvious that the people who scaled consistently, the ones who grew empires, redefined industries, and lived beyond limitations, all had these same elements, these 7 building blocks, in place. Some of them knew it. Most of them didn't. Many assumed their strength in one area was the key to their success, without realizing it was the hidden alignment of multiple strengths that made them unstoppable. And that's the danger. When we only see part of the picture, we assume the part is the whole.

One leader might credit their growth to discipline and consistency. Another might swear by their mindset or their relentless action. Yes, both of those things matter. But what I discovered is that they are just pieces of the puzzle.
To scale, not just once, but repeatedly, you need these specific 7 Building Blocks. Let's look at one real-life example and explore what I mean.

Most people think Oprah Winfrey's success comes down to mindset. They'll say it was her belief in herself, her vision, her ability to manifest what didn't yet exist. They're not wrong; mindset was a huge part of it. But look closer, and you'll see something most people miss or don't even pay attention to: she didn't just believe her way to the top, Oprah Scaled Up™ using the exact 7 Building Blocks I am talking about here.

She did it intuitively, without ever naming the process, or even knowing that there is a process. But she did it all block by block. Let's break this down further.

Support: She had **support** long before she had global influence, from mentors, like Maya Angelou to trusted teams who helped shape her vision into something scalable.

Mindset: She had the right **mindset.** She leaned into her trauma in order to learn all of the lessons and get the little gems which propelled her to the next level. This is the kind of mindset that rises after trauma, not just 'believes' through it. Her self-belief wasn't surface level, it was deep, and her support system helped her build it. Her mindset was forged in fire, rooted in meaning, and focused on service. However, it's almost impossible to have this mindset without the first building block - support.

Potential: She stepped into her **potential** over and over again. From a local anchor to a talk show host, then producer, CEO, media mogul, educator, and philanthropist—she never stopped asking, What else could I become? Note that none of these would be possible if she didn't have support and mindset behind her as a strong foundation. Can you see now how these build off of each other?

Small Steps: She took **small steps** every day. Consistency built trust, and trust built momentum. Her success wasn't one giant leap to stardom. It was one honest, intentional conversation at a time. Constantly moving forward and up.

Discipline: She applied **discipline** to everything. From the books she read before every interview to the operations behind Harpo Studios, Oprah ran things with structure. She didn't just speak from the heart, she executed like a professional. This discipline was possible because of the previous building block. It's extremely difficult to stay consistent when the steps are giant leaps.

Resilience: She embodied **resilience, grit,** and **tenacity**. She faced racism, sexism, abuse, rejection. She was told she wasn't fit for TV, but she kept going. Not because it was easy, but because the mission was bigger than the moment. She was able to sustain all of this because her prior building blocks were solid.

Results: Finally, she never stopped looking at **results**. Oprah paid attention to her audience, to the cultural moment, to what was working and what wasn't. She evolved because she measured. Because she measured, she stayed relevant.

So yes, mindset mattered. Her belief mattered. But mindset and belief alone don't build this kind of legacy. She lived the Scale Up™ blueprint. She just didn't call it that.

Oprah is just one real-life example of the **7 Building Blocks** in action, but these building blocks are present in every success story you've ever witnessed. They aren't habits. They're not personality traits. They are *structural elements*. If even one is weak or missing, the whole thing eventually begins to crumble. Without breaking things down into small steps, discipline becomes almost impossible to sustain. Without a strong support system, mindset falters. These building blocks don't just stack—they depend on each other. Each one must be strong enough to carry the next. When they're all strong and aligned? Growth becomes predictable, sustainable, and scalable. Because scaling isn't about working harder. It's about building better.

So what are the seven essential building blocks of the **Scale Up Blueprint™**? We'll go deeper into each one in the chapters ahead, but here's a high-level look at the foundation we're about to build.

Building Block #1: Support

Success isn't a solo pursuit. Scaling up requires people—mentors, allies, teammates, truth-tellers, and visionaries. I've seen too many brilliant people stall out because they tried to do it alone. They thought asking for help made them look weak. They thought needing support meant they weren't strong enough.

Strength isn't doing everything yourself. Strength is knowing who to bring into your world to lift, challenge, sharpen, and expand you. Your next level lives in your next connection, your network, and your support system. Until you learn to build the right circle around you, you'll keep hitting the same ceiling over and over again.

The research backs it up. A Harvard Business Review study found that leaders with strong social support networks are 2.4 times more likely to be rated as high-performing by both peers and supervisors.

According to Gallup, employees who feel supported by their manager are 70% less likely to experience burnout and 59% more likely to stay with their organization.

Finally, an MIT Sloan study revealed that startup founders who received mentorship grew their companies 3.5 times faster and raised 7 times more funding than those who didn't. Across industries, the data tells the same story: **support isn't just a soft skill—it's a scaling strategy.**

Building Block #2: Mindset

You can't scale a life, business, or mission beyond the limits of your thinking. Your mindset is the gatekeeper to every next level you dream about. If you believe growth is dangerous or risky, you'll unconsciously sabotage opportunities. If you believe success is scarce, you'll settle for less. If you define setbacks as failure, you'll stop the moment it gets hard.

But when you shift your mindset, when you reframe resistance as a signal of growth and challenge as a portal to possibility, then everything changes. Because once your mind expands, your life can too.

The science is clear: mindset isn't just motivational—it's measurable. In a groundbreaking study at Stanford University, psychologist Carol Dweck found that individuals with a growth mindset, or the belief that abilities can be developed, consistently outperformed those with a fixed mindset, even when starting with less skill or experience.

In addition, a 2019 study published in Nature found that growth mindset interventions led to significantly improved academic performance, especially among students facing adversity.

In the workplace, research from McKinsey & Company shows that companies led by executives who embrace adaptive, growth-oriented thinking are more innovative, resilient, and likely to outperform their peers.

Mindset doesn't just change how you feel—it changes what you do. What you do determines how far you can go.

Building Block #3: Potential

Most people are walking around with only a fraction of their power activated. They focus on what's obvious, what's already been validated, and what they're comfortable doing. In doing so, they leave massive reservoirs of potential untapped. Your greatest strengths may still be dormant. Your most valuable contributions might be buried under fear, doubt, or past failure. Scaling up means unearthing the parts of yourself you haven't yet used and learning to wield them with intention. This building block isn't just about doing more. It's about becoming more.

Studies show that we routinely underestimate our own capabilities. Research from the University of Pennsylvania's Wharton School found that people often don't recognize their "hidden talents" until challenged by new environments or external encouragement.

A Gallup strengths report revealed that individuals who identify and actively develop their natural talents are six times more likely to be engaged at work and three times more likely to report an excellent quality of life.

Lastly, a study in the Harvard Business Review concluded that high-performing leaders often have "latent leadership traits" that only emerge when they're placed in unfamiliar or high-stakes situations.

The truth is, most of your potential is still waiting on the sidelines. **Scaling up isn't about chasing more, it's about unlocking what's already inside you.**

Building Block #4: Small Steps

If I've learned anything on this journey, it's this: big leaps rarely change your life. Small actions, done consistently, always do.

People get overwhelmed by scaling because they think it requires dramatic overhaul. But sustainable growth is built through tiny steps taken with relentless consistency. Small, strategic actions compound. They build momentum. They create wins that stack on top of each other until, one day, you look up and realize you've scaled something extraordinary. This isn't about doing everything at once. It's about doing the right thing every day.

Science confirms what experience teaches: small, consistent actions drive exponential growth. A landmark study published in the journal Behavioral Science & Policy found that micro-habits—tiny, intentional behaviors repeated daily lead to significantly higher long-term success than dramatic goal-setting alone.

In the business world, James Clear's research-backed work on habit formation reveals that even a 1% improvement each day can lead to a 37x increase over the course of a year. This principle, often called "the compound effect," is rooted in neuroscience: small, consistent actions create lasting neural pathways through a process called long-term potentiation. Over time, these micro-habits rewire behavior and decision-making at the identity level. Clear emphasizes that massive results don't come from radical overhauls, but from tiny actions repeated relentlessly—whether that's sending one more follow-up, refining one sentence in a pitch, or making a single better decision each day.

Scaling isn't powered by intensity. It's powered by consistency.

What this means for you is simple but profound. If you send one email every day to close a client, or carve out just 15 focused minutes to work on your most important project, you won't just make progress. With the principle of "the compounding effect" you'll create momentum. One small step a day doesn't feel like much in the moment, but over time, it's the very thing that separates stuck from scalable.

The path to scaling isn't made of giant leaps. It's built one powerful step at a time.

Building Block #5: Discipline

I'm a keynote speaker. I motivate organizations on a regular basis, but I also know that motivation isn't enough to keep going. Discipline is what gets you to the finish line.

Too many people rely on bursts of inspiration. They move when they feel excited. Once the excitement fades, so does the work, and therefore the progress. People who scale don't rely solely on motivation. They build systems that make consistency automatic. They create routines, rituals, and environments that support execution. They don't depend on willpower. They engineer success.

If you want to Scale Up™, you must trade chaotic hustle for structured progress. Otherwise, your ambition will eventually burn you out.

Research consistently shows that discipline, not motivation, is the strongest predictor of long-term success. A widely cited study from the University of Pennsylvania found that self-discipline was more important than IQ in predicting academic performance, future achievement, and even happiness.

For example, neuroscientist Dr. Andrew Huberman emphasizes that the brain is wired for habits, not willpower, and that building systems, like consistent sleep cycles, work cues, and environment design creates the conditions for sustained success.

The most successful people aren't the most motivated. They're the most consistent.

Building Block #6: Tenacity

Scaling is not smooth. It's messy, unpredictable, and often painful. You will fail. You will face resistance. You will question whether you have what it takes. That's where this building block becomes everything.

Resilience is the muscle that grows when everything falls apart, but you keep going anyway. Grit is the fire that keeps burning when motivation fades. Tenacity is the refusal to stop, even when no one else believes, but you keep climbing.

Every person who's scaled anything significant has had to develop this. Not once, but over and over again. Because perseverance isn't a phase. It's a way of life.

Resilience isn't just a personality trait—it's a skill that can be built, strengthened, and practiced. Angela Duckworth, psychologist and author of Grit, found that grit—defined as passion and perseverance toward long-term goals—is a stronger predictor of success than talent, IQ, or even social intelligence. In one of her most cited studies, Duckworth followed West Point cadets through their first year, a notoriously grueling experience. Surprisingly, it wasn't physical fitness or test scores that predicted who made it through—it was grit. Cadets with the highest grit scores were 60% more likely to complete the training.

She then expanded her research to include Fortune 500 leaders, teachers in under-resourced schools, and finalists in national competitions—and found the same pattern: the people who succeeded weren't always the most gifted. They were the ones who kept going long after others quit.

If you've been waiting to feel ready, confident, or perfectly qualified before taking action—you're misunderstanding what real success is built on. It's not talent. It's tenacity. It's the willingness to stay in the game. To show up again. And again. And again. Resilience isn't just something you have—it's something you choose.

In a world full of fast starts and quick quits, grit is what keeps you climbing. Resilience is what keeps you in the game.

Building Block #7: Results

You can't grow what you don't measure. Scaling isn't just about doing more, it's about doing better. That means tracking what works, adjusting when things don't, being brutally honest about your results, and agile enough to pivot when needed.

People often confuse stubbornness with strength. But you don't want to be stubborn. You want to use your data and measurements to adjust in the right direction, because the ability to adapt is what keeps you scaling up. Growth isn't linear. It's a dance between momentum and adjustment. Between execution and reflection. This building block ensures you never stop evolving.

High-performance organizations and individuals all share one trait: they measure what matters. A global study by PwC found that companies that regularly track performance metrics and customer feedback are five times more likely to make faster, more effective decisions—and significantly more likely to outperform competitors in both revenue growth and innovation. Why? Because data replaces guesswork. Tracking creates clarity. And clarity leads to momentum.

Further research from McKinsey & Co. shows that organizations with robust measurement systems are twice as likely to hit strategic goals—and are more adaptable in high-change environments. And in leadership development, the Center for Creative Leadership found that consistent feedback loops were directly linked to higher emotional intelligence, improved team performance, and long-term growth in executives.

If you're not measuring, you're not managing. And if you're not managing, you're not scaling. Whether it's your daily habits, revenue goals, or team morale, what you track becomes what you improve. And the people who evolve the fastest are the ones who are honest enough to look at the data—and brave enough to do something about it.

Scaling doesn't come from guessing - it comes from clarity.

When you measure what matters, you give yourself the power to evolve with precision.

Scale Up Blueprint
7 Building Blocks

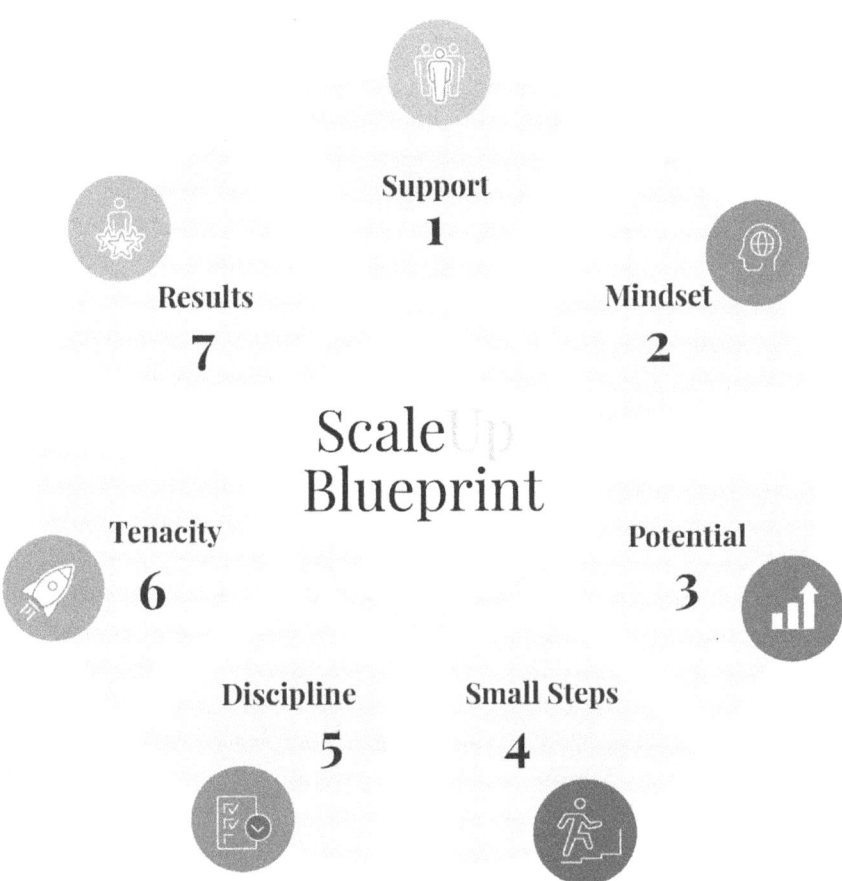

The Foundation Beneath Every Breakthrough

These seven building blocks are not optional. They are not "nice to have." They are the foundation of every sustainable success story you've ever admired. If you've been struggling, plateauing, or feeling like no matter how hard you work, you can't break through, it's not because you're not capable. It's because something in your foundation is missing or misaligned.

But don't worry, using **The Scale Up Blueprint™** you can identify what's weak and reinforce it, then the entire system becomes stronger. Scaling becomes simpler. Growth becomes repeatable. Your next level stops being a dream and starts being a strategy.

In the chapters that follow, we'll walk through each building block in detail. We'll explore real stories. Practical tools. Actionable shifts. Because you don't need more inspiration. You need a structure that works. Now, you are holding it in your hands.

Test The Scale Up™ System Yourself

The best part about this system is that it's not hidden. You can see it in action - anytime, anywhere. Try it right now: think of someone you admire. A wildly successful person. Then run the 7 Building Blocks against their story. Look closely, and you'll see that they've used every single one. Maybe not all at once, and maybe not on purpose, but they're all there.

Once you learn to spot these blocks, you'll begin seeing them everywhere. Even more powerfully—you'll notice where someone might be missing one. Look at someone who has "failed" and you will see that they are missing one or more of these essential building blocks.

Practicing this on others helps train your eye. Because let's face it, it's often easier to spot gaps in someone else's journey than our own.

But as you practice this, your awareness grows, and something shifts. You will start noticing your own gaps. Your own strengths. Your own patterns. And when you do? You gain the power to strengthen any block and scale everything in your life with greater clarity and intention.

"Behind every empire, every breakthrough, every reinvention, are seven invisible forces at work:

Support. Mindset. Potential. Small Steps. Discipline. Tenacity. Results.

These aren't optional. They're foundational.

Miss one, and the system wobbles.

Align them, and growth becomes inevitable."

Scale Up^{TM} Blueprint

Shareable Content:

Your Turn:

Success isn't luck. It's built, one block at a time. So here's your challenge:

Pick one person you admire. Run their story through the **Scale Up Blueprint™**. Which blocks are clearly visible? Which might be missing? Then turn that lens inward. Where are you strong—and where can you reinforce your foundation?

Share your insight with #ScaleUpBlueprint. Let's learn, grow, and build better—together.

Social Media Ready:

Scaling up isn't about doing more. It's about building better. Success comes from 7 foundational blocks—used by the world's top leaders, even if they don't know it. #ScaleUpBlueprint

Everyone sees Oprah's mindset. But behind her empire is a system: support, discipline, small steps, resilience, and more. Success isn't magic—it's structure. #ScaleUpBlueprint

Discipline gets you through when motivation disappears. Support keeps you strong when mindset wavers. Scaling isn't about a single strength—it's the synergy of all 7. #ScaleUpBlueprint

Chapter 4

Building Block #1 – Support: Leveraging Support & Strategic Networks

No one scales alone.

If there's one myth that keeps talented people stuck, it's the belief that scaling up is a solo pursuit. Inherent in that belief is the assumption that the key to success is grit, determination, and outworking everyone else. If you just hustle hard enough, you'll make it. Yes, all of those are important, but that's not how scaling works.

No high-level performer, fast-growing business, or transformational leader got there alone. Not one. Howard Schultz had Bill Gates Sr. Malala Yousafzai had Ziauddin Yousafzai. Every transformational figure had a mentor who expanded their thinking, offered guidance, and helped carry the vision forward. Every top CEO, athlete, and innovator had a circle—mentors, allies, advisors, collaborators. People who helped make the ascent possible. Despite that truth, most people still try to do it all themselves. We are still taught to wear independence like a badge of honor. We are told that asking for help is weakness. That being "self-made" is something to aspire to.

But there's no such thing as "self-made." Scaling up is never a solo game. It's always a team effort! Plus, the higher you climb, the more your success depends on the strength of the people around you.

That's why Building Block #1 of the Scale Up Blueprint™ is **Leveraging Support & Strategic Networks**. Without this foundation, every other block becomes harder to build. In fact, it becomes impossible. This is the block that carries all the others. If it crumbles, so does everything else.

Why Scaling Up Is Impossible Without Support

People often ask how I scaled from absolutely nothing—no money, no resources, no roadmap—to building a life, a business, and a mission in a country where I didn't even speak the language. Today, I live a life most Americans, and many people around the world, only dream of. "How did you get through everything?" they ask. "How did you scale up from zero to where you are now?" The answer is simple: I didn't do it alone.

From the outside, my success might look like it belongs only to me, because there isn't one person you can point to and say, 'That's who made it happen.' But the reality is that my support system wasn't just a backdrop—it was both the foundation and the launchpad for everything I built.

This doesn't mean I didn't work hard. It doesn't mean they "did it for me" or that someone told me what to do. It definitely wasn't easy. I still had to figure things out. I still had to do the work. It was terrifying at times. But what made it possible, what made it bearable, was that I had support. That strong, steady foundation gave me the courage and capacity to keep moving forward.

Before we go any deeper, let me share a simple truth backed by research: children who grow up with strong parental or familial support are significantly more likely to take healthy risks, explore, and develop resilience. In a national U.S. survey, only about 40% of children aged 6–17 displayed all three core flourishing traits—curiosity, perseverance, and calmness under challenge. And the single most consistent predictor is a strong relationship with at least one caring adult.[1] Research shows that a strong relationship with at least one caring adult is one of the most consistent predictors of resilience, even amid adversity. Why? Because when you have a support system—a safety net—it's okay to leap. It's okay to face your fears, because someone will be there to catch you if you fall. When it becomes okay to face fear, you get comfortable with it. You learn to assess risk, to stretch yourself, to try again. The earlier you experience this, the more solid and confident your internal foundation becomes.

For me, I was lucky, because I had that from the start. I had a strong support system as a child—and I still do. I never thought about it much and assumed that everyone had the same thing. It wasn't until I started asking the deeper question: *Why do some people scale up while others don't?* that I realized not all people are lucky enough to have such a strong support system like I did, which is for growth and scaling.

Adults who grow up with, and continue to have, strong familial support are significantly more likely to thrive in their personal and professional lives. According to Harvard's Center on the Developing Child, having at least one stable and supportive adult relationship is the single most common factor linked to developing resilience—even amid serious adversity. That resilience, built early, carries forward: shaping confidence, decision-making, and the ability to take healthy risks throughout adulthood.

And the corporate world is starting to take notice. Employer-sponsored childcare, for example, has been shown to generate ROI ranging from 200% to over 400%, driven by stronger employee retention, improved productivity, reduced absenteeism, and better workplace engagement

---

1. Source: Bethell, C., et al., 2019. "Positive childhood experiences and adult mental and relational health in a statewide sample." JAMA Pediatrics.

overall.[2] These kinds of support systems aren't just "nice to have." They're investments in sustainable growth—at both the personal and organizational level.

Without realizing it at the time, growing up in Yugoslavia gave me an incredibly strong support system—not just from my parents, but from my aunts, uncles, cousins, and friends - the entire community that was around me. I was part of a tightly woven community, where you never felt like you were going through life alone. Everyone was connected. Everyone belonged. It wasn't always the same, or equal, or perfect—but it was strong, it was diverse, and it made you feel like you mattered. You may be unique, but you were a part of the bigger puzzle and you fit. If you've ever seen the movie "My Big Fat Greek Wedding," then you already know what my family is like. Loud, loving, chaotic, and completely inseparable. I have one brother and 19 first cousins, and growing up, they weren't cousins—they were siblings. We saw each other almost every day. We vacationed together, built homes together (literally, from the ground up), and went to school together. We did life together.

Because of that, I never felt truly alone. I never felt unsafe, even in moments that should've been scary. Whether it was learning to ride a bike that was way too big for me, facing my fear of snakes, or standing at the edge of a high cliff deciding whether to dive—I always faced it, because I was surrounded by people who believed in me. While things like swimming or jumping off high rocks might sound minuscule, they were the moments that quietly, powerfully shaped the foundation of who I became.

---

2. Source: Child Care Aware of America. The Business Case for Employer-Supported Child Care. https://info.childcareaware.org/

Also referencing: Center on the Developing Child, Harvard University. https://developingchild.harvard.edu

Let's explore one of those moments more deeply—the lesson of the river, and how it taught me to dive, not just into water… but into fear itself.

Growing up in Mostar—one of the hottest cities in the Europe—also meant growing up alongside the coldest river in the world: the Neretva.

Mostar is known for its famous Old Bridge, built during the Ottoman Empire, which still stands today as a symbol of our heritage and history. For hundreds of years, locals have held diving competitions from this bridge. Since 2009, Red Bull has hosted an international cliff diving competition there every year. The bridge and the river are more than just landmarks; they're the soul of the city.

The Neretva is famous not only for its special emerald green color or for being the coldest river in the world, but also for being extremely fast, unpredictable, and dangerous. Locals are very familiar with its dangers, and, as kids, we are taught not only about the river but also how to live with it. We learn how to respect it and how to move with it instead of against it. The river is filled with and surrounded by large rocks, caves, and boulders which make it very treacherous. The current can sweep you down quickly. You might hit a massive rock that's hidden just beneath the surface, or worse you can get caught beneath one and drown. Deaths in the river are not uncommon. They happen often to foreigners, but even locals, especially children, have succumbed to its power. My five-year-old cousin drowned in such an unfortunate incident in the very same area where my brother and I, along with my cousins, had to learn how to swim. It took only a second. He was with his sister, and she turned around for just a moment. He was gone. We will never know whether he fell in or if the river's current pulled him in, but he was gone. He was only found several days later by a fisherman.

As a result of hundreds of years living on this river, all of those rocks, boulders, caves, and even small sandbars in the river have names. This information is passed on through generations by word of mouth. So, if you want to meet a friend by the river, you can give them the name of the rock, and they'll know exactly where to find you. Every inch of that river was mapped into our memory. You could say, "Meet me at Big Eagle" or "I'll be at Whale's Mouth," and everyone would know the spot. This was one of the first, subconscious lessons in naming my fears and facing them. This scary, dangerous place that should have been feared—wasn't. It was respected, embraced, and studied, but never feared.

Despite my five-year-old cousin and others dying in that river, we were taught not to fear it. Because fearing it would only make it more dangerous. By going to the river—swimming, playing, diving—together with cousins, aunts, uncles, and parents, they showed me something deeper. They showed me that it was okay to be afraid. They showed me how to face my fears. Name them. Learn about them. Move toward them—not away. Because danger doesn't lie in facing something scary and learning how to manage it. The real danger lies in avoiding fear altogether. The most remarkable thing is that, not only were these lessons taught to me early on and subconsciously, but they were taught in a fun and safe environment. Surrounded by people who loved me. In the water. Under the sun. On the riverbank. It was a dangerous place, but it didn't feel that way, because I was supported.

My family and I weren't the only people on the river; the entire community spent time there. My family was just one of many. As a result, this was more than a place - it was a system, a school, and a rite of passage. Like all sacred things, it came with rules. Little kids were only allowed to swim in the protected pools near a specific part of the beach. As you got older and "better," you could venture into the main part of the river—but only with adults or kids older than you. Even then, you couldn't go far. You had to move carefully, from one rock to another, learning the flow, the rhythm, the danger, and how to navigate all of it together.

Eventually, you were ready for something that felt massive: swimming across the entire river. That center part of the river was wide, open, and fast. No boulders to rest on. No sandbars to catch your breath or rock to grab. Just cold, powerful current that could carry you away in seconds. That was the goal of everyone there — being able to swim across safely, while having fun, as though it weren't a big deal. As a kid, that seemed just like simple fun, but as an adult, I realized the progression was purposeful. If any accident happened, we would know what to do. We wouldn't panic or drown, but instead could comfortably use the river to our advantage.

Each new challenge—each bigger risk—was talked through with someone older. Your parents. Aunts. Uncles. Cousins. Friends. Those who had done it before. It was only when they told you, "You're ready," would you be allowed to move to the next challenge. And when they told you that you were ready, you believed them-but the final decision was always yours. Everyone respected that even if you have the skills to do something, you have to be mentally and emotionally prepared to face your fears.

I still remember the first time I swam across the river. It felt like I had conquered the world. Back and forth, again and again, I went. Each time getting a little stronger and more confident. Each time a little freer. Once I'd done that, I wanted the next challenge. I wanted to dive. Some of the rocks by the river were 40 to 50 feet high. Diving from them wasn't just thrilling, it was a graduation of sorts. But you had to earn it.

Just like with swimming across the river, with diving there were rules, too. First, you started from the shore. You learned how to dive with your arms extended properly—because if you hit a rock you didn't see underwater, that form could save your life. Once you mastered form, you moved to diving off rocks that were 3 or 4 feet high. Then 5 or 6. Then 8 to 10. Eventually, you reached the final stepping stone before the bridge: Gvozden.

Gvozden was the last and highest rock we could dive from. The only other thing higher is the actual bridge itself. The big daddy. This was the rock you conquered before you even thought about diving off the bridge. The bridge was 79 feet high. Unlike my brother, Arnel, I never had the desire to dive off it. He, however, dove off of it at just 16 years old, winning second place in that year's competition. But the year he won wasn't just any year. It was during the Bosnian Genocide. That year, the bridge had been bombed, and large pieces of debris remained in the river, making it even more dangerous. You couldn't just dive into the usual spots we knew were safe; you had to hit an exact, narrow, clear patch of water... from 79 feet in the air. And he did it.

But I didn't want to be the bravest. I just wanted to be part of the fun on the river. Even though I was deathly afraid of heights, and still am, I really wanted to dive from all the rocks on the river banks. It looked fun. Joyful. Like flying and leaping into the emerald clear waters. So I watched. I watched hundreds of people do it—successfully—over and over again. I studied their moves. Memorized the takeoff. The landings. The sounds. The silence before the splash. Noticing all the eyes on the diver to make sure he or she were okay. And one day... I decided to try it. I knew I might fail. I knew I might get hurt. But I wasn't alone, and I trusted my support system when they told me that I was ready. I had the skills. I just needed to be brave enough to do it.

I was surrounded by people who loved and supported me. People who had done this before. People who would catch me—if not physically, then emotionally. They showed me how to do it. Encouraged me. Warned me what not to do. Little by little, with their guidance, I climbed higher, until reaching the highest rock.

That's where I learned what it really means to face fear. It's not about pushing through recklessly. It's about moving forward when you know you're supported. Even now, I'm still afraid of heights, but if there's water in front of me... I'm not. Because I know I'll be okay. I conquered heights over water, and no one can take that away from me.

That lesson didn't just let me have fun in the Neretva. The confidence I gained stayed with me. It allowed me to leap from high piers into the ocean. Even—on one wild occasion—from a hotel terrace into the Adriatic Sea. When you grow up learning to face fear with love and support all around you— you don't just take the leap, you learn how to fly.

Sure, I could have learned to swim and dive in a pool with lessons, structure, and safety rails on my own. I would've figured it out, but it wouldn't have been exhilarating or unforgettable. It wouldn't have taught me the most important lesson of all: the power of a support system. This wasn't just about swimming or diving but growing up surrounded by people with different perspectives—different personalities, different fears, different strengths. Some were scared like me. I could talk to them, share my fears, and feel understood. Some were experienced and confident—they'd done it a hundred times and knew what to expect. I could learn from their wisdom. Some were fearless dreamers. They didn't even see the danger. Just the thrill.

Being able to see all of those perspectives and choose: who I talked to, who I learned from, who I listened to - that was the real gift. It gave me options, mirrors, and the chance to grow into someone who didn't just survive fear, but learned how to move with it.

That kind of environment also taught me something equally important: discernment.

When you're surrounded by a wide range of people, you also learn, safely, who not to follow. The manipulators. The naysayers. The jealous. The reckless. You gain experience by interactions that prepare you for the future. At the river I was exposed to people who pushed too hard too soon, and some that wanted to hold me back, and some that just wanted to be better than me and tried to trip me up as a result. As a result, I didn't just learn how to swim across the river or dive. I learned *discernment*. I learned how to sense energy. How to recognize real support from shallow opinions. That one lesson alone would serve me for the rest of my life and is the reason why I am able to continually scale up.

"You don't just take the leap — you learn how to fly."

Ass a result of that lesson, when I was injured at sixteen and had to deal with tremendous fears, obstacles, and challenges, I already had a foundation. I didn't panic. I didn't spiral. I knew what to do. I used the same mindset and structures that have already been burnt into my persona to navigate all challenges. Just like I'd learned to navigate the river—one rock at a time, with people around me who would catch me—I knew I could navigate this, too.

When I arrived in the U.S., still a kid, without my family, without even speaking the language, facing a completely unknown world... I wasn't afraid. I hadn't arrived empty-handed. I had the tools. I had the memory of what it meant to build and have a support system, and that memory made me feel safe. Even though the people I knew weren't there, support still was—in a new form. Just like my parents hadn't personally taught me to swim across the river, others had stepped in. The same was true now in the U.S..

A group called Veterans for Peace saw my evacuation on the news and chose to help. Doctors believed in me. Teachers slowed down so

I could understand. Mentors stepped in, not because they had to, but because they wanted to. They didn't just give me advice. They gave me belief. They opened doors I didn't even know existed. They offered their networks, time, and care. Every one of those moments, those relationships of support, shifted the trajectory of my life. I still had to do the work. I had to learn to recognize, accept, and appreciate support. I had to know how to use it. I still had to face my fears and do the hard work. But once I did, every person became a resource. Someone to learn from and lean on who made scaling possible.

I've seen this same pattern everywhere—again and again. People and organizations that reach extraordinary levels of growth aren't always the smartest. They're not always the most experienced or best at their craft. They're the ones with the strongest support systems. They surround themselves with truth-tellers, growth-expanders, and strategic allies. They form partnerships, seek mentorship, learn from every interaction.

So if you want to scale up—whether it's your life, your team, or your organization— start here. Build a support system. One that helps you face fear, teaches you, and grows with you. One that celebrates with you when you finally swim across your river and feel like you've conquered the world.

How High-Growth Organizations Use Support to Scale

There are countless examples of organizations that scaled, not just because of visionary leadership, but because of the support systems they built around that vision. Apple didn't rise on Steve Jobs' brilliance alone. They cultivated a culture of innovation. They nurtured rising leaders. They formed strategic alliances and cross-industry partnerships that fueled momentum. Same with Salesforce. It wasn't just Marc Benioff's innovative idea of cloud-based CRM that made Salesforce into a global tech leader—it was the support structures he built around that idea from the beginning.

When Benioff launched Salesforce in 1999, he went beyond simply trying to build a better software product, he was building a movement and changing industries. And he knew that to scale something that ambitious, he couldn't do it alone. He built a support ecosystem across four critical dimensions: people, systems, culture, and community.

He started by surrounding himself with top-tier talent. Benioff hired executives and engineers who had deep experience in enterprise tech—people who could execute fast, adapt quickly, and anticipate the needs of arge-scale clients. But the magic wasn't just in who he hired. It was in the systems he put in place to support them. From the start, Salesforce was built with a multi-tenant architecture—which allowed it to scale seamlessly across thousands of customers without spinning up separate systems for each one. That decision, though technical, was a support structure—one that saved time, reduced costs, and enabled exponential growth.

At the same time, Benioff created an internal rhythm of alignment that most startups skip. He implemented **V2MOM** (Vision, Values, Methods, Obstacles, and Measures)—a strategic planning process that made sure every employee, at every level, was aligned to the same mission. This wasn't just goal-setting—it was operational scaffolding. It gave everyone a common language and a north star. And that alignment became a major advantage as the company scaled. With clear methods and transparent metrics, teams could move faster because they weren't second-guessing the path forward.

But perhaps most importantly, Benioff didn't see support as just an internal function. He extended it outward, into the community, the nonprofit sector, and the global innovation ecosystem. He pioneered the 1-1-1 philanthropic model—donating 1% of Salesforce's equity, product, and employee time to charitable causes. This wasn't just a fantastic PR move. It created a values-based network of impact partners, nonprofit users, and community advocates who supported Salesforce's brand from the outside in.

Benioff built support and and infrastructure—technical, operational, and emotional—that could carry massive scale. From internal alignment tools to global partner ecosystems, from cultural rituals to developer platforms, every layer of Salesforce is a support system designed to hold the company steady as it rises.

Salesforce grew because Benioff built the right scaffolding—and then invited the right people to help build the rest. That's what support looks like at scale.

*"Up to **42% of voluntary employee exits** could be prevented with better managerial support, but nearly half of departing employees report no proactive check-ins in the three months before leaving"*

The Fortune 500 isn't filled with solo acts. It's built on teams, cultures, and communities. Ecosystems that multiply impact and stabilize growth, much like the one I had on the river. This pattern holds true in startups just as much as in global corporations. The stronger your support system is, the greater your success. Vision is essential, but vision alone doesn't scale. Support does.

One of the clearest examples of what a strong support system can do is Taylor Swift.

Her success is directly tied to the people who've supported her from the very beginning. How many little girls dream of becoming a global superstar like Taylor Swift? So what made the difference - why did Taylor make it?

While many factors contribute to her success, one of the most important is: she had unwavering support—starting with her parents. As a child, then teen, and even now as an adult, Taylor has been surrounded by people who believed in her, invested in her, and stood by her every step of the way. Her mother was there when she was young, walking beside her through every challenge. They moved to Nashville as a family as a way of supporting her, but also to create a larger, laser-focused support network for Taylor. They paid for demo tapes. They faced every fear as a team—one step at a time. Throughout this time, Taylor still had to do the hard work, face her fears, and overcome obstacles. She was able to do all of it because she knew that behind her, she had a strong foundation that had her back.

Her Eras Tour broke records worldwide. To get there, I have no doubt that each step she took was terrifying—new, public, massive in scale. But she did it - and she never faced any of it alone. Even when Taylor enters a completely new environment—whether it's moving to Nashville as a teenager, or sitting across from movie executives to distribute her concert film directly to theaters, bypassing traditional Hollywood studios—she doesn't shrink. She doesn't go into survival mode. She builds support around her.

So how does she do that?

She starts by knowing who she trusts—and she keeps those people close. Her parents, her brother, her team—these aren't just industry hires or background characters. They're part of her inner circle. People who've been with her from the beginning. People who know not just her career, but her character. She surrounds herself with those who believe in her vision and share her values. And that allows her to scale in a way that still feels grounded, even when everything around her is growing at lightning speed.

Taylor has also learned how to delegate without disconnecting. She empowers her team to handle the mechanics while she focuses on the message. She's not micromanaging every detail—but she is choosing her collaborators with intention. Her creative director. Her stylist. Her publicist. Her dancers and crew. Each one is aligned not just with her brand, but with her energy. She builds trust, loyalty, and longevity into her business. And in turn, they give her the freedom to take bold, artistic risks—knowing that the foundation underneath her is solid.

One of the most moving examples of how deeply Taylor trusts and relies on her support system happened after years of fighting to buy back the rights to her master recordings. She had tried again and again—unsuccessfully—to regain ownership of her own music. And after several failed attempts, she made one final effort. But this time, she didn't send a legal team or high-powered attorneys. She could have. She could've hired the best of the best to battle it out.

Instead, she sent her mother and her brother.

It wasn't a power play. It wasn't a strategic threat. It was trust. It was love. It was family. And it worked. Her mom made the call afterward and said something Taylor will never forget: "I think you're getting your music."

That moment wasn't just about a business victory. It was a full-circle example of what real support looks like. It was a daughter being seen, protected, and believed in by her family. It was a long-fought battle ending, not with a courtroom win—but with a mother's voice on the phone saying, "I think it's yours."

That's what happens when you don't try to do it all alone. When you build a life and a business rooted in support—not just strategy. When you scale with people who care about you as much as they care about the outcome.

Much like I did when I came to the U.S.—a new country, a new language, a world I didn't understand.

Once you know what a support system feels like and how to use it, you can walk into any unknown and still find your footing. You're never starting from scratch, you're applying the same rules that helped you rise before. Taylor doesn't just adapt, instead she expands and reaches, creating safety around her to allow her to constantly scale up, and take the next big leap. She's the only musician to become a billionaire based on music alone, not through makeup or alcohol brands, but through the power of her craft and the strength of her support.

And then, very generously, she gives back to that system. Her dancers, her truck drivers, and her crew are some of the highest paid in the industry. Not just monetarily, but in other ways as well. She often bakes cookies, and takes care of people in humane ways to show her genuine care, because she knows the significance of her support system.

What's especially powerful is that Taylor sees her fans as a part of that support system, and she treats them as such, with reverence, gratitude, and love. She treats them not just as an audience, but as collaborators—part of the story, part of the success. She doesn't draw a hard line between "us" and "them." She sees them. She thanks them. She invites them in.

Taylor turns every album release into a shared experience—a treasure hunt of easter eggs, cryptic messages, and hidden clues. She weaves riddles into music videos, hides secret dates in liner notes, and drops breadcrumbs across social media that lead her fans down winding paths of discovery. It's not marketing—it's intimacy. It's her way of saying, "I trust you to find me here." And every time her fans decode a message or spot a pattern, they don't just feel like spectators—they feel like co-creators of the journey.

She recognizes that without them, none of this would be possible. And that recognition, which is rooted in deep awareness, is why her fan base is one of the most loyal and powerful in the world. Taylor Swift didn't learn this skill later in life. It's in her bones. Like me, she grew up in a strong, safe, emotionally intelligent support system, so she knows how to create, sustain, nurture, and, most importantly, grow one. The bigger your support system, the bigger your success.

For me and Taylor relying on this support system is almost like breathing. We don't even think about. Unfortunately, many people aren't that lucky. They don't grow up with the safety to trust others, surrounded by unconditional love, endless support, or the emotional blueprint to know how. When you don't know what safety feels like, it's easy to get burned. You mistake manipulation for support. Once you've been betrayed, it's hard to try again. You aren't even sure whether you are on the right path because none of is familiar.

It's not that those of us who grew up with support don't ever get manipulated. During my life, I have been taken advantage of plenty. I saw how often others took my kindness as weakness and have been burnt. I've been discriminated against, bullied, lied to, taken for granted, manipulated, and much more. But none of it could ever stop me from moving forward.

Even Taylor has been taken advantage of - by managers, industry executives, and so-called allies. Sometimes she won. Sometimes she got hurt. But, the most important thing is: she never stopped. She didn't let fear define her.

She faced it, with the help of her support system, again and again…until she won. That's how she changed the music industry. That's how she re-recorded her albums. That's how she reclaimed her entire catalog and took ownership of her voice and power. She had done things that no artist has ever done and continues to break barriers and records.

Another powerful example of support in action is Sara Blakely, the founder of Spanx. Yes, she had a brilliant idea, but the turning point wasn't the product. It was the people. She actively sought out mentorship. She built strategic relationships. She surrounded herself with people who could help her rise. It was when Oprah featured Spanx as one of her "Favorite Things," that it launched the brand into national recognition. But that moment didn't come out of nowhere.

Sara had cultivated her network long before it paid off. She reached out, connected, and asked for help. She stayed open and built her support system. She reached out, connected, asked for help. Early in her journey, every hosiery manufacturer she called said no… except one. That mill agreed to partner with her because its owner's daughters believed in her vision. That leap forward was made possible by trust, willingness, and a bit of vulnerability. From there, she continued building relationships at the grassroots—talking with department store staff, making her product a conversation piece. She credits much of her success not to being the smartest in the room, but to building the right room around her. "I didn't know the answers," she said, "but I knew I didn't have to do it alone." And that's the key.

If you want to predict whether a business will scale, look at its support structures. If you want to know whether a leader is ready for the next level, look at who's standing beside them. You'll have your answer.

The 3 Types of Support You Need to Scale

Scaling isn't just about working harder, it's about being supported smarter. That's why it's important to understand the three distinct types of support every person and organization needs to scale. Each serves a different purpose, and all three are essential.

People like Taylor, or like me, naturally push outward and expand our support systems in these ways. But for most, it doesn't happen by instinct, and that push has to be intentional and strategic. Let's break down these three types of support.

As you read, consider which ones you already have and which ones you may need to strengthen or seek out. This isn't just about getting help or filling up empty spots; it's about building the foundation that will hold you as you rise.

1. Strategic Mentors – Learning From Those Who've Already Scaled

These are the people who've already done what you're trying to do. They've climbed the mountain you're standing at the base of. They've stumbled, fallen, regrouped, and found a way to the top.

Mentors aren't just people with advice; they're people with perspective. They've made the mistakes you haven't yet made. They've weathered seasons you haven't lived through. Because of that, they can help you navigate more wisely, efficiently, and boldly.

When I think back to the river, these were the people who had already dived from the highest rocks. They were the ones who showed me how to extend my arms, how to look for hidden dangers under the water, and how to jump with both courage and care. They were also the ones who said, "You've got this," when I wasn't sure I did.

Mentorship isn't just about hand-holding. It's about expanding what you believe is possible—because someone else has already done it and is willing to show you the way. Sometimes, they don't even have to say much. Just their presence, certainty, and calmness in the face of things that terrify you is enough to anchor you.

When Oprah began her career, it was Maya Angelou's wisdom that became her anchor. She turned to her not just for encouragement but for grounding. Maya helped Oprah navigate the emotional complexity of fame, pressure, and influence, all while keeping her identity intact. Without that mentorship, Oprah's trajectory may have still been impressive, but it wouldn't have had the same soul.

Mentors remind you not just how to rise, but who to be as you do. So take a moment and ask yourself:
Who already lives at the level I want to reach?
Who has faced what I'm facing and walked through it?
Who challenges me to think bigger and then shows me how?

When you find them, don't wait for the perfect moment to connect. Reach out. Ask questions. Be humble. Listen deeply. Most importantly, apply what you learn. Scaling doesn't mean reinventing the wheel. It means finding someone who's built it already, and learning from them. Even with their guidance, the journey is still yours. However, with a mentor, the path forward is clearer, safer, and far more expansive.

2. High-Impact Networks – Your Inner Circle Drives Your Outer Results

Your network is your growth environment. It's the invisible atmosphere around you: the emotional, mental, and energetic climate that either lifts you up or weighs you down.

Most people underestimate just how much their personal and professional relationships shape their trajectory.
In reality, the people closest to you influence everything around you - your ambition, your self-trust, and your sense of what's possible.

If you surround yourself with people who play small, who resist change, who scoff at dreams or dim your light, eventually, they will shrink your vision too. This doesn't just apply to business. It applies to everything else as well. Your emotional resilience, your creative energy, even your ability to make smart decisions. They're all deeply affected by who's in your space.

Think back to the river. These are the people on the beach that are cheering you on as you stand on the rock, heart pounding. They're not diving for you, but their belief in you is what changes everything. You look out at the water, and you don't just see fear. You see possibility, because they're holding a mirror to your strength.

These are your truth-tellers and expanders. The ones who clap for you not just when you succeed, but when you dare, regardless of the outcome. They are there to support you not simply for your victories. They're the ones who not only say, but show you that, "You can do it. We're here. We believe in you."

Please note that not everyone in your life will be this person. That's why you need to be honest. You need to carefully audit your circle and ask yourself honest questions:

Who brings clarity—and who brings chaos?

Who fuels your growth—and who drains your energy?

Who believes in your next level—and who only sees your past?

If you answer honestly, are there some relationships that you need to lose? The answer is very likely yes. We've all had to let go of people and relationships that were no longer serving us. Often the hardest part of scaling isn't the strategy. It's letting go of relationships that no longer serve your vision. It's stepping back from the people who feel familiar but keep you stuck and spinning in the same cycle. People you have outgrown.

Scaling up requires intention. You don't have to cut everyone out, but you do need to elevate the voices you listen to most. Prioritize the people who stretch your thinking, who expand your possibilities, and who remind you who you're becoming, not just who you've been. Your future is shaped by the five voices you hear the most. The higher you go, the more intentional you must become about who's rising with you.

You can't build something extraordinary in a room full of people who don't believe it's possible. You need to be surrounded by those who know it's possible and push you to go even further. These aren't just friends or colleagues. They're your lifeline. Your sounding board. Your energetic match for the future you're creating. With the right people beside you, you don't just grow, you soar.

3. Support Systems – The Hidden Force Behind Sustainable Growth

This is the quiet architecture beneath every great leap.

Support systems are the behind-the-scenes structures, the internal teams, repeatable workflows, daily rhythms, and operational foundations, that hold everything together while you grow. They're not always visible from the outside, but without them, everything falls apart under the weight of success. Most people think scaling means doing more. But the real secret to scaling is doing less of what drains you so you can do more of what moves the needle.

Think of it like diving off those high rocks again. When I was preparing to dive, I wasn't the only one involved. There were people stationed all around, watching the river, clearing the path. If a stray piece of wood floated into the dive zone, someone would pull it out. If a group of kids wandered too close to the rocks, someone would gently steer them away. That invisible system allowed me to focus fully on the dive. It gave me the freedom to trust the moment, because I wasn't worrying about the current or hidden dangers below.

My only job was to take the leap.

That's what a great support system does. It removes distractions. It handles the clutter. It gives you the space to rise. In business, this is no different. Take Howard Schultz, the visionary behind Starbucks. He didn't scale Starbucks into a global brand by brewing every cup of coffee himself and micro managing every action. He built a system, a culture, an infrastructure, and a team that could consistently delivers the same warm, reliable experience whether you are in Seattle or Singapore. He focused on vision, brand, and innovation. Behind him was a machine: trained baristas, operational protocols, inventory systems, real estate teams, technology platforms, and support staff, that allowed him to scale without burning out or bottlenecking growth. He created freedom through structure. That's the key: growth without collapse.

It's not just about moving fast. It's about moving *sustainably*. You can't do that if you're stuck micromanaging every task, juggling every detail, and trying to carry the entire weight of your vision alone. You need structure. You need rhythm. You need freedom within a framework. That's how you protect your energy. That's how you scale your impact. So ask yourself:

What am I still doing that someone else could do better or faster?

What tasks leave me drained, scattered, or creatively blocked?

What systems could I build today that would give me back time tomorrow?

Then act on it and fix it. Delegate what drains you. Automate what's repetitive. Systematize what's important. Without systems, growth becomes chaos. But with right systems, growth becomes inevitable. Just like that river dive, when the path is clear and safety is built in, you can stop second-guessing. You stop stalling, and you leap.

*"Scaling isn't about working harder.
It's about being supported smarter."*

Scaling Alone vs. Scaling With Support

Trying to scale alone is slow, painful, and unnecessarily hard. Trying to do it all—prove it all—carry it all—might look noble from the outside… But inside, it's exhausting. It's also avoidable. Scaling with support is faster, more sustainable, and let's be honest, a lot more fun!

Learning to swim and dive with friends and family in the river was exhilarating. There was laughter, encouragement, stories shared on sun-warmed rocks. These are stories we still talk about! We weren't just improving and learning, we were enjoying the process. We were connected, growing together. Now compare that to learning alone in a pool. Sterile. Silent. No one to cheer you on. No one to tell you it's okay to be scared, and that you're ready anyway. That's the difference.

This is exactly why **Leveraging Support & Strategic Networks** is the very first building block of the Scale Up Blueprint™. It's not optional. It's the foundation for everything that follows. If you skip this step... if you try to muscle your way through alone... Yes, you might still succeed, but it will take longer. It will cost more. Most importantly, it will burn more energy—emotionally, mentally, physically, than you ever expected. As a result, you will never reach your full potential.

Support systems and strategic networks aren't luxuries. They're not "nice to have." They are the architecture of sustainable growth. They catch you when you fall. They lift you when you're tired. They anchor you when fear creeps in. They amplify every win, because those wins are shared.

"75% of top executives credit their success to mentors, and 90% of employees with career mentors report high job satisfaction"

Looking Ahead

With the right people beside you, the climb becomes easier and safer. But even with the strongest team, the next challenge will demand something just as critical: your mindset. Because even with all the external support in the world, you won't scale if your internal narrative is keeping you small.

In the next chapter, we'll explore the second building block of the Scale Up Blueprint™: **The Power of Mindset & Reframing Challenges,** and how it unlocks growth, even when everything around you feels like it's falling apart.

Let's keep building.

- *98% of ALL US Fortune 500 companies have mentoring programs*

- *100% of the TOP 50 US Fortune 500 US Fortune companies have mentoring programs*

- *The median profits for Fortune 500 companies with mentoring programs were OVER 2X HIGHER than for those without mentoring programs*

- *Fortune 500 companies with mentoring programs were significantly more resilient against employee quitting trends*

- *Fortune 500 companies without mentoring programs had a MEDIAN DECREASE of 33% in their number of employees*

Checklist

Building Block - 1 Support

Leveraging Support & Strategic Networks

Quick Win Checklist:

- ✓ Identify three people in your network who can help you achieve your next goal.
- ✓ Schedule one conversation this week with someone whose perspective you value.
- ✓ Join (or re-engage with) one group, community, or event that aligns with your scaling goals.
- ✓ Identify one gap in your current support system and outline a plan to fill it.
- ✓ Offer value first: find one way you can help a peer, partner, or client without expecting anything in return.

Shareable Content:

Your Turn:

Look at your current support system.
- Do you have mentors who stretch your thinking?
- A network that fuels your growth, not your doubts?
- Systems that protect your energy and free up your focus?

If not, this is your moment. Start building. Start reaching.

Identify one person you admire and ask a question. Find one task you can delegate this week. Replace one draining voice with someone who lights you up. Support doesn't slow you down, it scales you up.

Tag someone who's helped you level up.
Use hashtag **#ScaleUpBlueprint** to share your story and connect with others who are building their dream with support—not struggle.

Social Media Ready:

The biggest myth in business and life? That you have to do it alone. You don't. You just need the right support system. #ScaleUpBlueprint

Mentors shorten your path. Networks expand your vision. Support systems protect your focus. Want to scale? Don't do it alone. #ScaleUpBlueprint

Apple, Amazon, Taylor Swift, Spanx…All scaled because of one thing:Strong, strategic support. #Leadership #ScalingUp

Audit your circle: Who brings clarity—and who brings chaos Who fuels your growth—and who drains your energy? Who believes in your next level—and who only sees your past? #ScaleUpBlueprint #MindsetMatters

---

Chapter 5

Building Block #2 – Mindset: The Power of Mindset & Reframing Challenges

"The way you see a challenge determines whether you break through it or break under it."

Maybe you're facing something hard right now. Maybe there's a goal you haven't reached, a setback you didn't see coming, or a problem that keeps resurfacing no matter how hard you try to solve it. If so, you're not alone. Regardless, what separates those who scale from those who stay stuck is not luck, intelligence or talent. **It's mindset.** That's where it all begins. In your head.

The most successful leaders, businesses, and individuals aren't the ones who avoid problems. No matter how hard you try to prepare, you can never avoid problems. The most successful people are the ones who reframe problems as opportunities. They use and see those problems not as setbacks but as a propellers to take them further. That's why Building Block #2 of the Scale Up Blueprint™ is mastering the **Power of Mindset**—and learning how to reframe challenges so they become fuel, not friction.

> *"Leaders with a growth mindset see 34% higher employee engagement and 47% higher team performance."*
>
> *Harvard Business Review*

SCALE UP BLUEPRINT

The Moment That Changed Everything

I was hanging out in a courtyard of our apartment building with five of my friends when a bomb exploded, killing all of them and severely injuring me. My brother, Arnel, was across the street in a different courtyard hanging out with his friends when it happened. He saw everything. The moment the bomb exploded, I didn't understand what was happening. My mind was still trying to catch up to reality. I scanned the scene in slow motion, looking around me in concentric circles, absorbing every detail, but not really comprehending it. Bodies. Blood. Silence. The warm air that smelled like gun powder. Sun shining.

It was a lot.

Then I saw my brother across the street. I saw him frozen in motion with terror in his eyes. In that moment, it was as if I left my own body and entered his. Through his teary eyes, I saw what happened. I saw that the rocket propelled grenade (RPG) exploded less than 10 feet from me, killing all five of my friends instantly. I was the only one still alive - barely.

Before we go on to the rest of the story, I want to sidetrack a bit and talk about perspective and positivity. Far too often we hear people about changing your perspective, looking at the glass half full instead of half empty. And far too often, I meet people who say that they are positive. I see them sharing all of these positivity memes on social media. But the real test of your positivity and ability to shift your perspective is not when things are going pretty good and you feel okay or even great. The real test of whether you are positive person, or can shift your perspective, happens when things aren't going well. When you world is falling apart, and you feel like you are losing every battle. When you feel like your world has been turned upside down, and there is no way out. That's when the true test happens.

It's how we react in those seemingly dire moments that determines our trajectory. How do you stay positive and shift your perspective in such moments — in moments when YOUR proverbial bomb lands in your lap? And how did I stay positive in this moment - the moment where I was sitting on the ground, bloody, injured, and barely alive. See, like you, I always have a choice. And back then, I had a choice too.

I could look to my left at my brother, hanging out with his friend in a courtyard 500 yards from me, and say: **Why me?** Why did this happen to me? I'm only sixteen. I didn't ask for this. I wasn't part of this war. This isn't fair. My bother and his friends are doing the same thing, and bomb didn't explode there. Why did I have to get punished? **I am a victim.**

Or I could look to my right, at the five dead bodies beside me, and say: **Wow! I lived!** I'm still here. I have a second chance at life. I owe it to them, and to myself, to make this life matter. I get to live my life now with a whole new appreciation and vigor. In this case, **I am a hero.**

Nothing about my circumstances changed. All of the facts remained exactly the same. The only thing that changed is my perspective. While the facts stayed constant, the meaning I gave them could be my own. And, with that choice, instantly, my life trajectory is different. I get to choose whether I will live out the rest of my life as a victim or a hero of my own story. No one else gets to decide this for me. That's the power of *reframing*.

You can be the victim of your circumstances or the hero of your story. You choose. The story you tell yourself will shape everything. And just like me, anyone—no matter their circumstances—can make that same shift.

"People who view stress as a growth opportunity rather than a threat have 43% lower mortality rates."

Stanford research, Dr. Alia Crum

If you choose to see yourself as a hero of your story, and are able to shift your perspective no matter what, then anything you do, anything you touch will be a success. Conversely, if you aren't able to do this, or do it partially, or do it only when things go well, or do it subconsciously, then, no matter what you do, your path will be extremely difficult and you will have a hard time reaching your goals. Even the goals you reach will be far less than your potential because doing something with a negative mindset is like digging a ditch with one arm tied behind your back. Yes, you can do it, but it will be extremely difficult and not reflective of what you could really achieve if you did it with both hands.

When it comes to mindset, there are many roadblocks we can encounter. Often we have blindspots, imposter syndrome, or tough situations where we are unable to clearly see the blessings. We do not believe that we are worthy. This will make it difficult to shift our perspective and move forward in a productive way. This dynamic is where your support system will help you, which is why that building block is crucial to implement first. With the help of you support system, you'll be able to shift into positivity and become the hero of your life.

Let's look into this second building block a bit further.

Why Most People Get Stuck at the First Roadblock

The difference between those who scale and those who stay stuck almost always comes down to how they interpret facts. As we saw with my story, facts can and do remain the same. What makes or breaks us is not our facts or our situation, but our view and interpretation of those facts. Which means the power to change how we respond to hardship lies within us. Unfortunately, most people see obstacles as stop signs. Something to get through unscathed. This aversion leads to a disempowering mindset that makes you fear failure, so you end up avoiding risk. You resist change or your ability to reach a full potential. A disempowering mindset looks like:

- Leaders who fear failure avoid risk—and their companies stagnate.
- Businesses that resist change and become irrelevant while competitors innovate.
- Individuals who take setbacks personally and stop themselves before they ever reach their full potential.

High performers, however, see obstacles as starting points and invitations to grow. They realize that these obstacles are showing them opportunities for improvement. They are being shown areas for growth that will make them better, more diverse, and constantly keep innovating. These are all necessary ingredients for scaling. Because, scaling isn't about avoiding difficulty—it's about seeing it differently, and then using it to your advantage.

While mindset work is a big enough topic that it could be its own book, below are three simple mindset shifts that will help you stay on track and live like a true hero of your life.

SCALE UP BLUEPRINT

The 3 Mindset Shifts That Will Help You Stay On Track

There's a moment in everyone's journey where something hard hits, and the mind reflexively says: *This is too much. This is impossible. I'm not cut out for this.* Our instinct is to retreat. To run the other way and avoid pain. Let's face it, our primal brain is trained to avoid pain and seek pleasure, so this isn't a surprise. But what's important to know is that it is in those moments -not in the victories, not in the applause - that growth begins to reveal its deeper shape. This is where the real work begins: stopping that primal brain from instinct and acting with intention. Moving forward beyond survival.

People who scale aren't necessarily the ones who had more talent or resources. Often, they were the ones who made these three simple but powerful shifts in the way they thought about and approached obstacles. I've seen these three mindset shifts transform not just businesses, but lives.

1. Move From Conclusion To a Question:

Go From "This is impossible" (Conclusion) to "How can I make this work?" (Question)

Most people meet a challenge and make a conclusion about it. They say: "I can't because…" "It won't work because…" or even "I can do X goal" All of these are conclusions. When you live in the conclusions, you have already decided the limit — you will make that happen. Henry Ford famously said, "You either think you can or you think you can't, either way, you'll be right." This doesn't apply only to your ability to do something, it also applies to how much of something you can do. How far you will go is determined by the way you think. So if you think you can reach X, Y, and Z, then that's where you will plateau. What you need to do is move away from conclusions, and live in question. What all is possible? This removes any limitations.

When people hit a wall or an obstacle, they may try a little…but then they walk away. Sometimes they interpret it's a sign. A closed door. A message from the universe that maybe this isn't meant to be. Which is why you'll hear things like: "I can't afford this." "I don't have the connections." "This just isn't realistic." They start looking for excuses, reasons to justify the outcome they want. The easy, comfortable outcome. They get into what psychologists call **confirmation bias.** Seeking out information to prove that the decision they made is the right decision. This is a sure way to lie to yourself and decline without even realizing it.

But those who scale, they hear the same voice of doubt. However, they then ask a question. Instead of "Can I?" they ask, "How can I?" Instead of "I can't afford this," How can I afford this? Instead of looking at the wall and backing away, they look for a foothold. A crack. A lever. A way to shift the structure. They are constantly scaling and evolving moving from the conclusions into questions, like "How can I…?" And, what else can we dream up? What is possible?"

This is why the "crazy" dreamers always reach goals that seem impossible. They constantly live in the questions, and limitations for them are just illusions. If we look at some of the recent developments, Elon Musk is a great example of someone who did live in a conclusion that the entire aerospace industry believed — it's too expense for private efforts. It all started with a question, the right question - "How can we make this possible? "How can we reduce the costs by 90%?" And today, private space travel is affordable enough that folks like Katy Perry are traveling to space for fun. Whether you like or don't like Elon Musk or Katy Perry, the reality is that the entire industry was revolutionized because of that one question and a simple mind shift. This is what I call the engineer's mindset. It's not about ignoring limitations, it's about designing around them.

Use this in your life:

Try removing "I can't" from your mental vocabulary for just one week. Replace it with:

"How might this be possible?"
"What would need to happen for this to work?"
"Who could help me figure this out?"
"What else is possible?"

Whether in your professional team or your family, try noticing when the conversation gets stuck in limitations and conclusions, and gently redirect it to possibility. To a question. You'll be amazed how quickly people rise to the level of the questions you ask.

2. Redefine Failure

People who scale big often fail bigger. Those who don't understand failure may see it as something really bad. But if you redefine failure as data, then you realize that you never failed. As a result, that failure never defines you, because you've trained yourself to see it differently.

Most people treat failure as evidence of who they are. It hits personally, especially if you are a C-level executive, managing people, departments, or organizations. Failing can feel like a personal failure, and it quickly turns into "I failed." That thought unfortunately then translates to "I'm a failure." That kind of conclusion makes the risk and pressure of scaling up even greater. So it's safe to stop trying, and keep smaller and more comfortable.

But what if failure wasn't a verdict… and was just data?

When Thomas Edison was asked about the thousands of failed prototypes before inventing the lightbulb, he replied: "I didn't fail. I just found 10,000 ways that didn't work." He didn't see any of the times he tried as a failed attempt, he saw each of them as a lesson. Data. A piece of information that pushed him to the next try. That mindset isn't just optimistic—it's essential. Because when you're building something bigger than you've ever built before, you will mess up. You will be wrong. That's not the end, it's the curriculum. It's information for you to use.

There is a selling strategy that's been successfully implemented where the goal of a sales person is to get to as many no's or rejections as quickly as possible. There are two reasons why this is valuable approach. First, sales is often the numbers game — if you can sell 1 unit every 100 tries then the quicker you get through your 99 tries, the faster you'll reach your sales. The second reasoning is that with each rejection, you are learning new information and improving your strategy, so you start recognizing signs early on who is a potential and viable client, versus one that will never buy. This learning makes the process even faster, getting you to your goal with less stress and more results, quicker.

In this approach, failure is redefined as data. You are using that information to get better and better, which means you've never really failed, you've only learned. Once you are able to redefine your relationship with failure as one of data and useful information, you will then be able to keep moving forward objectively, learn as you go, and keep scaling up beyond anything you can imagine. What you saw as failure, you now see as a helping hand. Information that helps you navigate in the right direction. (I hope you can see why it's almost impossible to redefine failure as data without first having and mastering the previous building block, of having the right mindset and being able to view any situation in a favorable way.)

Use this in your life:

Next time something falls apart, whether it's a project, a launch, or a conversation, ask:

- "What did I learn here that I couldn't have learned otherwise?"
- "What is this showing me about my process, my systems, or my assumptions?"
- "How can I make this better and do better next time?

When failure becomes feedback, you stop shrinking, and start adapting. And that's how growth accelerates.

"Entrepreneurs who reframe failure as feedback are 3x more likely to pivot successfully and achieve long-term success."

Failory Startup Data Report

3. Do Not Retreat - Train

Move from "This is too hard" to "This is training me to be stronger."

Some challenges feel unfair. Overwhelming. Brutal. Trust me, I know. Life has dealt me things no human, let alone a child, should have to face. When things get difficult, it's only human to want to retreat. It's our innate instinct to retreat from discomfort that kept us alive for thousands of years. But this instinct was built for the survival of the human species, not our own growth. Here we are learning growth and scaling up, not survival. We need a different set of tools for growth. Retreat is also easier than facing hardship and trying over and over again. As a result, people give up, stay the same, and don't grow beyond their comfort zone.

But those who do scale up-they become friends with hardship. They don't look at difficult times as a sign to retreat, they see it as a training ground. They go in and know it will be hard, it will be difficult, but we must train. That's how we get better.

Every difficult client, every rejected proposal, every sleepless night, it's not just something to survive. It's something that's sculpting you. You have to see it as your coach. NFL players aren't necessarily having fun during training — their practices are often grueling. They are getting their team ready for the big game. These challenges you face aren't there to make you retreat, they are your punching bags, your laps to run, hurdles to jump, fall, and scrape yourself up. All of it is there to train you for your big game. Recognize that it's hard, That you are growing, and that it's all preparing you for your big win.

"Employees who believe challenges are "training" report 57% greater resilience and 40% more satisfaction with their work."

American Psychological Association

Howard Schultz pitched his idea for Starbucks to 242 investors before someone finally said yes. Can you imagine hearing "no" two hundred forty-two times... and still believing in your vision? This is like a runner practicing laps and jumping over 242 hurdles. That's not just perseverance, it's reframing pain as preparation.

Each "no" was training him to pitch better. To hold his vision tighter. To face rejection without crumbling. The next time you see a Starbucks, remember: someone had to be told "no" 242 times to bring that cup of coffee into your hands.

Use this in your life:

The next time something feels too hard, ask:

- **"How is this training me for the next level of who I'm becoming?"**
- **"What qualities is this challenge strengthening in me?"**
- **Imagine yourself in a virtual workout room and know that this is a part of winning.**

Transformation lives not in being fearless, but in choosing a better frame for the fear. It lies not in being perfect, but in seeing an obstacle differently. Your most difficult chapters might actually be your most valuable ones. In fact, most of the time, that's the case. That's where your resilience is being built, not in theory, but in real time.

Let these mindset shifts become your internal compass. Not just when things are easy-especially when they're not. If I could go back in time and redo my entire life again, I would still go to that courtyard, wait for that bomb to explode, and go through every single thing that happened to me. I would erase nothing. Not because I am some kind of masochist that wants to live in pain, but because I know that it was these difficult times that gave birth to the biggest lessons, and let me find the depths of myself I never knew existed. Things I would never trade or give up. Lessons that are priceless and make my life far better. Things that no one can take away from me.

The same goes for you. During your most difficult times, you will discover and learn things that will be get you to the depths of yourself you never knew existed! You will gain priceless gifts that will forever expand your mind, heart, and existence, which will help you to keep scaling up, no matter what.

Survival Tools vs Growth Tools

Scaling is 80% mindset and 20% strategy. You can have the best business plan, the best talent, and the best tools in the world, but if your mindset isn't aligned, you will sabotage your own growth. Mindset is the foundation. It's the lens through which you see the world. The limit of your next level will always be the limit of your thinking. So if you want to scale, train your mind to reframe:

- Resistance as refinement.
- Challenge as opportunity.
- Setback as setup.

"You can't use survival tools to create growth. What kept you safe won't take you forward."
— #ScaleUpBlueprint

This is how you begin to lead yourself differently—and how you lead others through adversity. The ripple effect is real: when leaders adopt these shifts, their teams and organizations rise with them. A study by DDI found that 85% of leaders who underwent training reported increased team member engagement. Additionally, 82% of their direct reports noted enhanced team productivity.

In order to do this, we must understand the difference between survival tools and growth tools. As I mentioned before, nature wired us to survive, but if we are just surviving we are not growing and we need a different set of tools. You cannot use your survival mindset tools to create growth. This is why most people end up struggling. They try to use survival tools to achieve growth, and it doesn't work. Here are the three examples that will help you see the difference of growth mindset tools versus survival mindset tools.

1. Crack Open

Survival Tool: The seed's hard outer shell protects it. It keeps the seed from being crushed, dried out, or eaten. That shell is essential for survival.

Growth Tool: The outer shell now must crack open. The very protection that kept it safe becomes the thing that must be broken in order to expand.

Growth requires vulnerability. It requires risking what the seed has always known, so roots can go down and new life can emerge. The instinct to stay closed might have been useful in a storm, but it will kill you in a greenhouse. Allow yourself to be vulnerable and open so you can keep growing.

2. Pick the Right Tool

Survival Tool: A firefighter. When your house is on fire, you need a firefighter. Their job is to put out flames fast. This is survival mode. You want them there, and you want them there fast. But once the fire is out? You won't ask that same firefighter to help you design your dream home. Or build it.

Growth Tool: An architect. A new blueprint. A new skillset. When you are ready to build your new house, you will call an architect and a contractor. Building requires an architect's mindset. You have to stop reacting and start designing. You have to shift from "What do I need to do right now to stay afloat?" to "What do I want to build for the future I'm here to create?" This shift is hard, because survival tools often masquerade as productivity. These tasks make you feel like you're doing something important: working overtime, staying vigilant, putting out fires. But growth requires different tools and asks you to slow down. To think longer term. To take bold, creative risks.

3. Let Go of the Fear

Survival Tool: Emergency brake. Survival instincts are like the emergency brake in your car: they're meant to slam on when you're heading toward danger. To save you. That's useful when you're skidding or about to crash.

Growth Tool: Gas pedal. But imagine trying to drive to your dream destination with the emergency brake on the whole time. Just halfway down, for safety. You'll burn out the system. You'll burn out. You'll feel frustrated. You'll wonder why it's so hard to move forward when you're pressing the gas with everything you've got.

Scaling up means learning when to release that brake and press the gas. Not because there's no risk, but because now you're driving with intention, not reacting to fear. It's not that you're weak. It's that your instincts are conflicted, and while one foot wants to fly, the other is still trying to keep you safe.

That's why one of the most courageous things you can do in your journey to scale... is to release the brake. Trust the road beneath you. Let go of the emergency mindset. Give yourself permission to design, not just react. Because the future you're building, doesn't need a firefighter with the e-brake on, it needs a visionary.

Looking Ahead

You've built the right support system. You've started to shift your internal narrative with a healthy growth mindset. Now, it's time to unlock one of the greatest hidden forces behind breakthrough growth: **your untapped potential.**

In the next chapter, we'll explore **Building Block #3 – Unlocking Hidden Potential**—and show you how to harness strengths you didn't even know you had.

Let's keep building.

Checklist

Building Block - 2 Mindset

The Power of Mindset & Reframing Challenges

Quick Win Checklist:

- ✓ Identify three people in your network who can help you achieve your next goal.
- ✓ Schedule one conversation this week with someone whose perspective you value.
- ✓ Join (or re-engage with) one group, community, or event that aligns with your scaling goals.
- ✓ Identify one gap in your current support system and outline a plan to fill it.
- ✓ Offer value first: find one way you can help a peer, partner, or client without expecting anything in return.

Shareable Content:

Your Turn:

You've now seen how a single mindset shift can reshape your entire path forward. **So ask yourself:**

- Where have you been using survival tools to try and grow?
- What limiting "conclusion" are you ready to replace with a better question?
- What failure could you reframe as data or training?

Write your answers down. Keep them somewhere visible. And share one of your new reframes using the hashtag #ScaleUpBlueprint. **Let others know that you're not surviving anymore—you're scaling.**

Social Media Ready:

Mindset isn't fluffy. It's foundational.
You can have the best tools, the best plan, the best team—but if your thinking isn't aligned, you'll sabotage your own growth.
#ScaleUpBlueprint

You're not weak for wanting to retreat. You're human. But survival tools aren't growth tools. Let go of the emergency brake. Start building instead of just reacting.
#MindsetShift #ScaleUpBlueprint

The facts don't need to change—*your lens does*.
Reframe the story, and you change the ending.
#GrowthMindset #ScaleUpBlueprint

Some people stop at the first "no." Others keep going until the 243rd becomes their YES. That's not hustle. That's a mindset built for scaling.
#Resilience #ScaleUpBlueprint

Chapter 6

Building Block #3 – Potential: Unlocking Hidden Potential

Your full potential isn't something you find. It's something you uncover.

We've been taught to look for potential like it's buried treasure, something hidden deep beneath the surface, waiting for the right moment, the right person, or the right conditions to be discovered. But what I realized is that potential doesn't live out there in some distant future or some perfect version of life. It doesn't even live outside of you. Your potential lives *inside* of you. It's there right now. You don't have to do anything to create it. It's always been there, and it will always be there. So, you don't go looking for it outside of yourself. Rather, what you need to do is look within.

"Over 85% of innovation practitioners say that fear often or always holds back innovation—but fewer than 11% of organizations do anything about it."

Fear is a natural barrier. Yet, true unlocking of potential comes when you lean into it—every. single. time.

Your potential is already inside you, quietly waiting, like a spark waiting for oxygen. Not passive, not dormant, just waiting for permission. Waiting for you to stop searching outward and start clearing away the dust of fear, doubt, and outdated beliefs. It is waiting for you to start looking inward. Unlocking your potential isn't about discovering something new. It's about removing what's been holding you back so what's already there can finally rise. Your full self isn't something you become. It's something you unleash.

The Moment That Forced Me to Ask: Why Am I Still Here?

After the bomb exploded, five of my friends were gone in an instant. I was the only one left alive. But surviving that moment was only the beginning. My body was torn apart. I had lost massive amounts of blood. Quite soon, infection was raging in my body. There were no medications, no proper medical care, and no reason—medically or logically—that I should have lived.

And yet, I did. I lived when I shouldn't have. I recovered when no one thought I would. I kept going forward, even as nagging questions crept quietly through the back of my mind. Questions that haunted me for years: **Why me? Why am I still here? Why was I the only survivor when I was the closest to the bomb, and the most exposed? What did it all mean? Did I have a bigger purpose? Was I wasting my life?**

At sixteen, I didn't have the answers. I couldn't even begin to sort it all out. But one thing I knew for sure was that if I was still breathing, it meant something. It meant that I couldn't just waste this life and the opportunity I was given. The least I could do was try my best to reach my full potential and get the most out of this life, this precious gift that so many take for granted. And so, I began asking myself deeper questions:

- **What does a full life actually look like to me?**
- **What strengths have I ignored because I was afraid to see them?**
- **What would I regret if my story ended tomorrow?**
- **What might be possible if I stopped letting fear shape my future?**

I assumed that, as I worked through these questions, a clear path would appear in front of me, showing me the way to my highest potential, happiness, and a fulfilling life. But that wasn't it at all. In my simple quest to answer those questions, I realized that living your full life and reaching your full potential is not about finding a path forward, a path to follow, or set of steps to take. It's really about removing the limits and beliefs we've placed on ourselves. Limits like, fear, assumptions, inherited beliefs, quiet doubts we never speak out loud, or even our subconscious thoughts that run our life. These are the true barriers to our potential, not a lack of talent or resources.

Once you start removing this emotional debris—like taking shackles off a bird—you'll begin to feel freer, and your ability to fly will reveal itself to you and the world.

The Truth About Potential

Most people think of potential as a ceiling, or something to reach, and, once you hit the top, you are done. But it's nothing like that. Potential is like a series of infinite doors. Each time you step into discomfort, take a risk, or question an old belief, you open a new door. What's on the other side of each door? More of you. More ability. More depth. More impact. More strength. Here's the best part: you can open as many doors as you want. There is literally no limit. There is always something to learn, something to expand, and something to conquer.

You are limitless in your imperfections, which means you are *also* limitless in your potential. And that, my friend, is the beauty of life. You can spend as much of it as you want digging around, expanding, scaling up, and growing. This makes your growth and scaling up infinite. The only thing that can and will stop you is you deciding how much is enough to make your life full. Living this way makes you feel like you lived a full life, so on your deathbed you can say: "Wow, that was a fun ride. I did a lot. I don't regret anything. I milked every bit of life that I could." This reminds me of my Great Dane, Rosie.

I got Rosie when she was just a few months old. She was missing a leg and wore a prosthetic from the time she was a puppy. When she was just a couple of weeks old, her Great Dane mom—a 135-pound gentle giant—accidentally stepped on her tiny foot and broke it. The vet never prescribed antibiotics, and the injury became infected, forcing her leg to be amputated. From that point on, Rosie wore a prosthetic. In those early months, we had to make her a new leg almost every month because she grew so quickly.

From the very beginning, I knew I wanted Rosie to live her best life. To reach her potential and be the absolute best she could be. I didn't know exactly what that meant, but I knew I wanted it for her because it was the same thing I wanted for myself. There was no reason she should get anything less out of life than any other dog—or any other being.

Thankfully, I had the time, money, and energy to give her what she needed. I changed my entire life around Rosie, and made sure she would experience as much life as possible.

Despite having a prosthetic leg, Rosie completed service dog training and became my service dog. She also completed agility training. She trained at the same facility where K-9 dogs are trained. She jumped over obstacles, A-frames, and completed every task that was put in front of her. She and I drove across the country countless times—east to west, north to south—exploring as much as we could.

She met almost every animal: cows, sheep, horses, dolphins, birds, dogs, cats, squirrels, ducks, and many more. I deliberately drove her to places where she could experience different air temperatures, smells, and terrains—different from Florida, where we lived. She swam in lakes, rivers, oceans, the Gulf, and waterfalls. She played fetch in the Mojave Desert and rolled in the snow at the Grand Canyon. She walked in a Mardi Gras parade in New Orleans and chased sea gulls under the Santa Monica Pier.

The only rule I had was this: if she was interested in something, I would allow her to explore it and teach her how to enjoy it. If she was having fun, I knew we were on the right path.

Rosie even learned to paint. She painted and sold nearly 200 original paintings. It all started one day when I was painting a large piece on the dining room floor. Rosie kept getting into my paints and interrupting me until I finally said, "Fine, if you want to paint, you'll have to do it yourself and leave my stuff alone." I created a makeshift paintbrush she could hold in her mouth—a simple brush with crepe spreader extensions to form a T-shape. I put a canvas in front of her and prepared to teach her. I even set up a camera to film it, expecting the training process to take days.

But I was completely wrong. She needed no training. She simply picked up the brush, walked to the canvas, and began to paint. I wasn't even ready with the camera. But it didn't matter. It wasn't about the painting. It was about the joy. She just did it, without prompting or instruction how to do brush strokes, or where the paint should go. Whatever came out was perfect, because it came from a dog who was simply having fun.

The more I got to know Rosie, and the more in tune I became with her, and the clearer it became what she wanted to do next. Rosie passed away just two months shy of her 10th birthday. It's her passing that carries the deepest lesson - a lesson I want to pass on to you.

A few months before she passed, Rosie had a regular vet visit. Her bloodwork was excellent. The vet said her labs looked like those of a four-year-old puppy. I was ecstatic, thinking we had years ahead of us—maybe she'd become the longest-living purebred Great Dane.

But then, one day, she lost control of her bowels. She tried to get up, but fell. She was devastated—embarrassed, shaking, looking at me with the saddest eyes I've ever seen. She only calmed down once I had cleaned everything up.

After talking to the vet, I wasn't concerned. He said this was a normal stage for elderly dogs. The vet said she could live like this for years, and to me, that didn't matter. I had already made a plan: towels, blankets—whatever it took. I would walk this next stage with her.

The following day, it happened again. But this time, I wasn't home. When I arrived, Rosie had crawled across the floor just far enough to tuck her head under a chair—to hide in shame. I rushed to clean her, to comfort her.

I don't know exactly what happened that night, but something shifted. I could feel Rosie starting to slip away. It's like she decided that she was done. That she had lived out her best life, drained everything she possibly could out of it, and now it was time to move on and complete this cycle.

The next day, she stopped eating. I made her go out, but I knew it was only out of obedience, not desire. She drank a little water. Otherwise, she just lay there, shallow breathing, quiet and still.

The vet prescribed pain meds, but I had no reason to give them to her. She wasn't in pain. She just stopped. Curled up in our favorite snuggle spot, she barely moved. Not knowing what was happening, I cancelled all of my plans - work, life, all of it - and lay on the floor beside her, waiting for something to reveal itself. Two days ago, she had been vibrant. Now she was fading.

The morning came. I tried again. I offered her some food, she wouldn't eat it. I tried to get her to go outside, but she didn't want to move. So I decided to listen to her, as I have all those years before. I knew she would tell me what she needs. Right then, she wanted me to sit on the floor with her.

And so I did. I laid on the floor next to her as she was slowly breathing petting her favorite spot on her head, between her eyes, as I whispered sweet nothings into her ear. Then, suddenly, she moved. She got up, gently shifted her body across mine, rested her head on my chest, curled around my neck… took one final, deep breath… and passed away. It was one of the most beautiful things I've ever witnessed. She showed me the same peace and grace in death as she did in her life.

Rosie lived a full life. She lived out her full potential, and the moment she realized she was no longer able to do this, she transitioned peacefully, completing a cycle in a healthy, graceful, and beautiful way. She didn't fight it. She didn't hang on. She had no regrets. That was her final gift to me.

I don't know what happens after we pass. Is she in rainbow heaven, passed into a new life, or still hanging out with me in some energetic form—I can't answer those questions. But I don't need to. Because what she left me with was the lesson that I will always carry within myself, which I want to share with you.

Live so fully that when it's time to go, you're not afraid. You're ready. You've done enough. You've been enough. You've experienced enough. That's what it means to reach your potential. That's what it means to live without regret. And that's what I want for you. To reach your potential, to live your life so fully, to do and conquer so much, that when your final day comes, there are no regrets. You are at peace, looking back with pride and satisfaction.

To get to that place, you have to start now. Start uncovering your potential, conquering your fears, trusting yourself to move forward. Not just once, but again and again. Because that's how you scale up. That's how you keep expanding. That's how you get the most out of life.

How do you begin? Movement. You need to open that scary door and walk through it. Because potential is not passive. It's activated—by you. Only you.

"The way to scale is through motion. Potential doesn't activate on its own—it responds to you walking toward it."

My Greatest Fear—and the Moment I Took Control

So how do we activate this potential? How do we uncover it? In Rosie's case it was far easier because she didn't have limiting beliefs that she grew up with. She didn't doubt herself. She was free and open to life and the experiences. Another thing Rosie had was me — she trusted me and knew that I would never put her into danger or cause her any harm. So when she first faced an obstacle, she looked to me for approval, support, and reassurance. (By the way, this is why your first building block is so important - do you see how they all stack on top of each other?) Each time she faced her fears, she built more trust, not just in me, but also in herself. Until one day, she safely tested her limits on her own. At that point all I had to do is say no (if I felt something was too dangerous), and she would listen.

For us humans it's the same thing — it's just a lot more complicated because we do have limiting beliefs, we do have an inner voice narrating to us, and, often a "support system" that bogs us down. It's easy to confuse closeness with support. We often assume that just because someone has been in our life for a long time—family, old friends, coworkers—they must be part of our support system. But not all familiar faces are safe spaces. Some relationships exist by default, not by design. And if we're not careful, we mistake familiarity for alignment. True support isn't about who shows up often—it's about who shows up well. Who helps you grow, stretch, think bigger. Who believes in your evolution, not just your history. Building a powerful support system means learning to discern the difference. It means lovingly releasing what no longer serves, and intentionally surrounding yourself with people who help you expand, not shrink. Trying to navigate all of those can become complex and overwhelming. Still, no matter how complex it feels, if you want to reach your potential—you have to face your fears. You have to go directly into them, get familiar with them, explore them, and make them your friend. Like Rosie, once you do this enough times, you'll start trusting yourself and your support system to keep going and each time it will become easier to do.

One of the fears that lived with me long after the war was my fear of flying. I've always had a fear of heights, but my first helicopter ride made this far worse. A couple months after my injury, I was evacuated from the war zone. Part of evacuation was a helicopter ride to a nearby hospital. During this ride I was strapped to a stretcher in a military helicopter.

The doors were open on both sides. I lay strapped to a tiny stretcher, secured by a single thin seatbelt. It didn't feel safe at all.

As the helicopter took turns and tilted, I felt like I was going to slide and fall out. I was badly injured, so I could only hang on to the seatbelt with one hand hoping that if I did start to fall, my one working arm would be strong enough to keep me in. I remember holding onto that seatbelt so tightly, ridden with fear. I remember the wind. The shaking. The open sky. The loud noise. I remember thinking that at any moment, in a split second, I could fall out and be gone.

That memory got etched into my nervous system. For years, flying brought me anxiety, panic, and a sense of losing control. I flew when necessary, but never without dread. I would get anxiety days before the flight, full panic on flight day, and then relief when I landed - but only for moments, because I knew the return flight was waiting for me. I didn't want to miss out on life because of my fear and not travel, but it was a horrible way to live.

Until one day, I decided that enough was enough. I wasn't willing to let this fear define me anymore. I didn't let the fear stop me, but I also didn't conquer it so I can fully live. Like those days on the river, I knew that to conquer my fear I had to go right into it — and as a result, I did something most people wouldn't expect: I signed up for flying lessons. I didn't search for hypnotists or a therapist to help me get rid it - no. What I did is I leaned into it. Learned about it. Made it my friend.

When I showed up to my first lesson, I talked to my instructor about my fears. I explained I was facing this fear I had, and that I had no interest in becoming a pilot, I just wanted to reclaim my power. For the lesson, we flew a small Cesna plane, which felt much more like that helicopter ride etched in my memory than any commercial plane. This tiny plane didn't have AC and we were flying in Florida heat. To make matters worse for me, the pilot asked that we leave our windows open. I was devastated. Window open on a plane? What?! I was scared to my core and told the instructor that I would likely have a panic attack in the air, in which case he would have to turn the plane around and land it.

Overwhelmed with fear, I was shaking going into that plane. But I knew that the best fight against my fear was knowledge. I asked him to explain everything as we went along. I learned tons about flying, aerodynamics, and a simple fact that flying over the trees is more turbulent because they release oxygen. He not only explained that fact, but he even flew through an area without trees to show me the difference firsthand. This built trust.

During the flight, I did have a panic attack, but I worked through it in the air because I felt I could. I kept pushing through, and welcoming all the fear, embracing these scary feelings, until the moment that the pilot said to me: "Hey, look over to your left." Which I did. I will never forget that sight. It was incredible. We were flying over the turquoise waters of Florida, with islands spread across like little jewels. White crescent beaches curving like moons. It was paradise. I couldn't believe it. I've seen sights like this flying from commercial plane, but they were usually obstructed views that lasted seconds, minutes at the most.

This was different. I had a 180 view of paradise. It was and remains one of the most beautiful sights I have ever seen. As I saw that, I immediately forgot about my fears and started looking around trying to take it all in. I wanted to carve it into my memory forever. Suddenly I felt the wind... coming from that open window. It wasn't scary like before. Now it was soothing and cooling and smelled like fresh salt in the air. I was ecstatic. I couldn't believe that I was so high up, in a tiny plane, not only fearless, but absolutely loving it. My first thought was, *I can see why people have private planes and get addicted to flying.* It's peaceful, beautiful, and calming.

Then came a moment I never expected—the pilot asked if I wanted to fly the plane. I felt intimidated, but at this point I learned to trust myself and the situation. It was time to deploy everything I learned and test it. Oh, I'll never forget the moment I took control of the plane for the first time. It was exhilarating. It was freeing. It was far beyond anything else I have ever experienced in my life. Now, the same fear that once made my hands shake and my breath short... became a source of joy, power, and freedom. I wasn't just flying a plane. I was flying through fear. On the other side of that fear, that door, I found a new version of myself. One that I never would have known existed had I not pushed past my fears. The very thing I feared the most became a pathway to my greatest strength.

This is what it means to walk through your fear, through your door, and discover your greatest strengths that lie there dormant, waiting for you.

"Potential isn't something outside of you. It's already inside—quietly waiting for permission to be unleashed."

This Is How We Unlock Hidden Potential

Whether you're an individual, a leader, or building a company, you need to know that you will never uncover your full potential inside the comfort zone. Growth lives on the edges. If you're not actively seeking those edges, you're leaving power on the table. Your untapped potential isn't hiding from you. **You're hiding from it.** It's in the difficult conversations you're avoiding. It's in the project you keep putting off because you're scared to fail. It's in the bold decision you haven't made yet because it might not work out. The edge of your discomfort is the doorway to your next breakthrough. If you're leading a team or an organization, the same truth applies to them. Your people have more to give than they realize. Your company has strengths it hasn't yet deployed. But you'll only find them if you intentionally build a culture that invites stretch, challenge, and curiosity.

Please note, that to fully discover our potential, we need the first two building blocks — our support and our mindset. Having those two will help us see the right doors, and walk through them so we can dig deeper, step into the challenge, and truly realize our potential.

A Real-World Example: Netflix's Leap Into Streaming

For years, Netflix thrived on its DVD rental model. It was stable, profitable, and it worked. But leadership looked beyond and asked, what could be? They saw a future not in red envelopes, but in digital streaming, and though it was unproven and risky, they chose to activate their potential, not cling to comfort.

Netflix didn't merely pivot, they disrupted themselves first. They harnessed their advantage in user behavior insights, combined with data-driven experimentation and relentless innovation. Their core strength wasn't DVDs; it was their ability to learn, iterate, and evolve internally.

The results speak volumes: from roughly 6 million subscribers in 2006, Netflix grew to over 301 million globally by 2025 . That kind of exponential growth didn't come from playing it safe, it came from leaning into discomfort and trusting that what they'd already built could power the leap.

What we are talking about here isn't just anecdotal, it's scientifically supported. A 2022 study in Motivating Personal Growth by Seeking Discomfort found that deliberately stepping into uncomfortable territory drove greater engagement and goal achievement compared to sticking with the familiar. Moreover, research on adaptive leadership shows that leaders who encourage experimentation, recalibration, and discomfort tend to produce more innovative, resilient organizations.

That is what potential-based leadership looks like. It's not about abandoning what's working. It's about building on it, bravely stepping through new doors and trusting that growth will follow.

3 Ways to Start Unlocking Hidden Potential

1. Choose discomfort on purpose.
Make it a habit to do things that stretch you. Not randomly, but strategically. Discomfort is the gym where potential gets stronger. Just like in the gym, the more you practice the stronger you get, and the easier it becomes.

2. Question your stories.
What stories are you telling yourself about who you are, what you're capable of, or what's possible? Most of them aren't true, they're just familiar.

3. Don't wait to feel ready.
You'll never feel 100% ready to grow. Do it anyway. **Action unlocks access.**

Reflection Questions

Unlocking hidden potential begins with honest self-inquiry. Start here:

- What fear have you been avoiding that might actually be an invitation to expand?
- Where in your life or leadership have you been playing small—and what would it look like to step into more?

Looking Ahead

Unlocking potential is powerful. But it's just the beginning. Because knowing your potential doesn't mean much unless you **act** on it. That's why in the next chapter, we'll dive into the power of micro-actions—small, intentional steps that compound into massive growth over time.

Transformation doesn't come from a single moment of inspiration. It comes from consistent momentum.

Let's keep building.

Checklist

Building Block - 3 Potential

Unlocking Hidden Potential

Quick Win Checklist:

- ✓ List three skills or strengths you haven't fully leveraged in your current role or business.
- ✓ Identify one area where you're underestimating your capabilities and commit to stretching it.
- ✓ Ask a trusted friend, colleague, or mentor what they see as your untapped strengths.
- ✓ Dedicate 30 minutes this week to learning or improving one skill that excites you.
- ✓ Remove one task or obligation that drains your energy and replace it with something that fuels you.

Shareable Content:

Your Turn:

Think of one area in your life or work where you feel a quiet nudge. Something calling you forward, but fear or uncertainty has kept you from acting. Ask yourself:

- What would it look like to follow that pull—even just one step?
- What "door" have you been standing in front of, waiting for permission to walk through?

Write it down. Say it out loud. Then take action—even the smallest one. Because potential doesn't bloom in stillness. It moves with you. #ScaleUpBlueprint #UnlockYourPotential

Social Media Ready:

Potential doesn't knock. You have to open the damn door.
#ScaleUpBlueprint #Leadership #MindsetShift

What if the thing holding you back isn't lack of talent—but a lack of movement?
#UnlockYourPotential #GrowthMindset

Rosie the 3-legged Great Dane lived a fuller life than most people—because she didn't wait for perfect conditions. She just showed up.
#Inspiration #LiveFully #ScaleUpBlueprint

The truth is: your potential isn't buried. It's just been waiting for you to get out of your own way. #PersonalGrowth #PotentialUnlocked

Chapter 7

Building Block #4 – Small Steps: The Micro-Actions That Drive Big Growth

Big results don't come from big moves. They come from the small, consistent actions no one notices.

We live in a world obsessed with big moments. The dramatic reveal. The viral launch. The overnight success. Scroll through social media or turn on the news, and you'll see highlight reels of achievements: standing ovations, massive deals, and before-and-after transformations. But what you rarely see is the nitty gritty that made it all happen.

Whether they talk about it or not, behind every breakthrough lies something far less glamorous: the are small, uncelebrated, and often invisible actions. The early morning wake-ups. The quiet commitment to keep going. The daily discipline when no one's watching. Sometimes it was as simple as showing up or keeping the lights on for another day. It is these tiny actions and small steps that lead to real transformation and genuinely scaling up.

No matter what the success is, it isn't one giant leap that changes everything. It is hundreds, sometimes thousands, of tiny steps taken when no one else is paying attention. Success isn't a sprint, and it doesn't show up in fireworks. Instead, it sneaks in through routine. It arrives in the unnoticed choices and the decisions to stay consistent, to recommit after a setbacks, and to keep moving even when motivation fades. Those are the real catalysts of growth.

That's why Building Block #4 of the Scale Up Blueprint™ is **The Small Steps** - Micro Actions that Drive Big Growth. The real transformation isn't in the moment everyone sees on social media; it's in the small actions they never see.

Believe it or not, even this building block, the one that seems the most straightforward, requires precision. If you don't go about it properly, if your small steps are misaligned, inconsistent, or reactive instead of intentional, you can quietly sabotage your progress. Those missteps may feel harmless in the moment, but over time, they can be fatal to your momentum, your business, or your career.

There's also a common trap here that you have to watch out for. What many people think are small steps are often big leaps in disguise. They underestimate just how small a micro-action really is and needs to be. So they push too hard, too fast, and burn out or lose motivation when results don't come quickly. Scaling up requires the right action, repeated with care.

Small steps can take you far but only if they're truly small, truly sustainable, and pointed in the right direction. Let's take a deeper dive into this building block.

Why Big Wins Aren't Enough to Scale

Most people believe growth happens in seismic shifts. They wait for the right time. The perfect conditions. The game-changing opportunity. That magic spark that makes everything click and their world suddenly changes. But if you're waiting for a big moment to save you, you'll spend your whole life waiting.

Big moments are rare. When they do come, they won't change everything (or even anything) unless you're ready, and you know how to sustain the transformation the big changes brings. Without the groundwork of small, consistent effort, without a foundation built on micro-actions, those breakthrough moments will slip through your fingers. You won't be able to hold onto them, let alone grow from them. The "big moment" will come. It will be exciting for a moment. Things may shift temporarily, and then it will pass, sending you back to the beginning.

We understand this concept through statements like "15 minutes of fame", or a "one-hit wonder". This is the reason why most lottery winners end up back back where they started. It wasn't their hard work, small steps, or micro actions that got them the big win. They are not equipped with the tools to handle their instant success, so they will lose it all. They didn't really scale up, and they won't automatically stay there.

Conversely, the opposite is true. If you use small steps and micro actions to scale up and earn millions, it doesn't matter if one day you lose it all, because you know you will get it all back relatively quickly. That's why many entrepreneurs and successful people will tell you that if they lost it all, they can get it back within a year or so. The reason is once you scale up, once you learn what to do and how, no one can take that away from you.

The people and companies that actually scale don't wait for something big. They know that the big win is coming IF they do the small steps and micro-actions in the right direction. So they move quietly, steadily, and deliberately every single day. They do the work when it's boring. They do it when no one's watching, when there's no guarantee of results. When the big win does arrive, it doesn't shake them. It's not even a surprise. It feels as natural as breathing. The best thing about this is that, because they've done the work and earned it from the inside out, they're able to not only hold onto it, but they can keep scaling up to the next level. Sustainable success isn't built in a single moment. It's built in a thousand quiet ones.

"Most people fail not because their goals are too big, but because their actions are too big to sustain. Tiny steps don't just move you forward — they keep you from falling apart."

Case in Point: Martha Stewart – Scaling Through Everyday Excellence

Martha Stewart become a household name and built her with decades of small, deliberate actions. Long before she became a global brand, she was a caterer in Connecticut, preparing meals from scratch, styling tablescapes by hand, and paying attention to every detail others overlooked. There was nothing flashy about her ascent, but it was consistent, thoughtful, and it created a reputation for her one small step and micro-action at a time.

Instead of waiting for a big break, she created it by doing small things with excellence over and over again. A newspaper column led to a book. A book led to television. Television led to product lines, brand partnerships, a magazine, and eventually, a media empire. Her rise was steady and built on a clear foundation: teach what you know, show up with care, and deliver quality again and again.

And then, it all fell apart.

In 2004, Stewart was convicted of insider trading and sentenced to five months in federal prison. Overnight, her name was dragged through headlines, her brand nearly collapsed, and her reputation was questioned by millions. But even there, behind bars, she didn't fall apart. She returned to what she knew: structure, habits, excellence. Stewart reportedly followed a strict daily routine. She made crafts, taught classes, and even redesigned elements of the prison's landscaping. She kept showing up for the work, even when no one was watching. Especially then.

When she was released, her rebuild wasn't dramatic. She didn't launch with fireworks or rebrand herself entirely. She returned to the fundamentals — to writing, to teaching, to cooking, to creating. To the same micro-actions that built her name the first time. Slowly, her credibility returned. Her influence grew again. Her business stabilized and then expanded because of the trust and consistency she had spent years compounding.

Martha Stewart's story isn't just about success. It's about infrastructure. It's about building something so solid, so deeply rooted in discipline and daily action, that even when everything is taken away, you still know exactly how to begin to rebuild and scale up.

That's what small steps and intentional micro-actions do. They don't just move you forward, they make you unshakable.

How I Turned an "Impossible" Goal into a Reality

Before my injury, I had my life planned out. I was going to be a professional athlete and there was nothing stopping me. Even though I was only in high school, I was already playing on professional city teams in a couple different sports. My entire life consisted of training. No matter what I did, whether it was school, chores, birthday parties, or even sleeping and eating, I just wanted it to be over so I could get back to playing sports. Basketball, volleyball, soccer, tennis - it didn't matter. Life was nothing but sports. Everything else felt like a nuisance that was in the way of what I really wanted to do.

Until my injury.

At that point, everything flipped. Just living to another day felt like a huge achievement. Running without working legs felt like an impossible fantasy. Despite all of that, I knew deep down I wanted to run and that some day, I would reach that seemingly impossible goal. I didn't know how, nor did I know how long it would take, I just knew that's what I was going for because I couldn't have imagined my life without running.

Knowing and believing I would run didn't mean that every day I tried to run (big move) — in fact, most days I wasn't even thinking about running. The mere thought of running scared me, because it was so overwhelming to try and imagine how will I ever get there. Actually, most of the things that happened and were necessary for me to run I would have never even been able to imagine. Who would have guessed that I first may need to get through over 100 surgeries, years of intravenous antibiotics, years of physical therapy, 15 years of hospital runs and surgeries, both mental and physical recovery, a Paralympic athlete, and a tailless dolphin to get there?

All I was thinking about is "What can I do today? How can I move that needle just a little bit towards my higher goal?". Some days, it was standing for thirty seconds longer than before. Some days, it was moving a toe. Some days, it was letting my body rest and heal, trusting that stillness was also a form of progress. I stopped chasing the finish line. I started chasing the next step. There was no timeline. I didn't know if it would take one year or fifteen. That wasn't the point. The point was forward movement—however small. Over time, the small steps became strides. The strides became strength. The strength became momentum.

The last time I had run, I was 16—running toward a bomb, toward what would become the greatest turning point of my life. Fifteen years later, I found myself preparing to run again, this time not from fear, but toward possibility. I was working with Brian Fraser, a Paralympic athlete and coach, who became my guide back into motion. He wrapped a belt around my waist and explained that running is really just controlled falling. I had never thought of it that way—but the moment he said it, something clicked. I was scared. I was fascinated. And I was in awe of the fact that three-year-olds somehow learn to do this without thinking. At 31 years old, I was terrified of falling. But Brian stood beside me. I leaned forward. And together, we started. Step by step, I began teaching my muscles what to do. I started trusting the ground again. I started trusting myself. The first few times I ran on my own, it felt completely foreign—the ground moved in ways I didn't remember, horizon was bouncing and made me a little motion sick, and my body wasn't sure how to respond. But slowly, with support and patience, I learned how to run again.

Eventually, I ran my first 5K marathon. But that race, the part most people see in pictures with me crossing the finish line with my arms up, wasn't the defining moment. The real breakthrough had already happened. It happened in the hundreds of days no one saw. In the thousands of moments when I chose progress over perfection. When I showed up for the process, even when it felt invisible and unrewarded. **That's the power of small steps and micro-actions.**

Real Life Examples

This methodology isn't something that's exclusive to me and my life. Others are successfully implementing this building block weather they realize it or not.

Consider the story of John, an individual I watched transform firsthand—we shared the same personal trainer, and over time, I witnessed him drastically improve his fitness by starting extremely small. Instead of trying to run long distances immediately, John set a micro-goal of jogging for just five minutes every day. This seemingly minor commitment was easy to stick to, yet it built consistency and confidence. Over time, John gradually increased his running time and endurance. The compound effect was remarkable – what began as a 5-minute daily jog eventually enabled John to complete multiple marathons, a feat that once seemed impossible. This case demonstrates how daily habits, even on a small scale, can accumulate into major personal achievements. The key was John's mindset of focusing on tiny, manageable steps rather than an overwhelming goal. By celebrating small wins (like simply lacing up and jogging each day) and staying consistent, he gained momentum. In the long run, those small steps literally carried him across marathon finish lines, validating the chapter's claim that consistent small actions lead to big changes.

This can also be applied to business and organizations. Let's look at Mailchimp, for example. Long before it became a household name, Mailchimp was just a side project built by two friends, Ben Chestnut and Dan Kurzius, who wanted to help small businesses send better email. There were no investors. No viral growth hacks. No big launch. Just slow, steady work.

They didn't try to "scale fast", chase headlines, or take venture capital to grow overnight. Instead, they showed up, day after day, improving the product, talking to customers, fixing bugs, answering support tickets, writing helpful blog posts, and refining one small feature at a time. None of this work was glamorous or big. But it was consistent, and it worked.

Over nearly two decades, those daily micro-actions compounded. Their customer base grew. Their team grew. Their software got better through quiet, persistent evolution. When they finally sold Mailchimp in 2021 for $12 billion, many people called it an "overnight success." But it wasn't. It was a 20-year build, brick by brick, with no outside funding, fueled entirely by discipline, consistency, and the belief that small steps, taken daily create big, lasting growth.

One of my favorite examples of this kind of sustainable growth is Toyota! They aren't just one of the largest automakers in the world, but they are also one of the most respected companies of any kind. Their secret isn't what most people think. It's not a revolutionary car model or a singular business decision. It's something much quieter and far more powerful. It's *kaizen*.

Kaizen is a Japanese philosophy that means **"change for the better"** or, more simply, continuous improvement. It's the belief that small, consistent actions taken every day can lead to massive long-term results. At companies like Toyota, kaizen isn't a project or a trend. It's a mindset woven into every corner of the business. Every employee, from the factory floor to the C-suite, is encouraged to identify small inefficiencies or opportunities for improvement and take action, even if that change is just a few seconds saved or a process made slightly easier. No dramatic overhauls. No giant leaps. Just tiny tweaks like moving a tool closer, shaving seconds off a process, refining the angle of a part.

In Toyota's West Virginia engine plant, a team noticed occasional camshaft chatter — a defect that would require halting the entire production line and disassembling faulty units. To prevent this, they invented a cam chatter checker: a simple tool combining an LED light, a whiteboard, and reflexive nylon. By shining the light on a camshaft and observing the shadows, operators could detect microscopic defects early. That tiny tweak eliminated costly shutdowns and saved the plant hundreds of thousands of dollars in a single incident. A seemingly minor tool — but one that prevents massive downtime.[3]

Alone, each change is almost invisible. But together, they create a system that is relentlessly improving. Over time, those micro-optimizations add up to higher quality, better efficiency, fewer defects, and more trust

---

3. Source: Toyota Pressroom, 2020

from customers around the world. Toyota doesn't chase perfection in one moment. They build excellence one small step at a time — every single day.

Why Small Steps Make Failure Safer

Another reason micro-actions are so powerful is because they make failure safe. When you move in small steps, even a wrong turn isn't catastrophic. You can course correct quickly without derailing your entire business or momentum.

Dropbox, now a well-known cloud storage company, began with a mindset shift in how to launch a product. Rather than spending years and millions (big move) building a perfect service, the team created a 3-minute demo video for a Minimum Viable Product (MVP) – a simple screen recording of how Dropbox would work, and shared it with early adopters before the full product even existed.

This tiny step, which required minimal time and effort, had fantastic results. The video cleverly included insider jokes for the tech community and clearly illustrated the solution Dropbox offered. It went viral, attracting a flood of interest. Overnight, Dropbox's beta waitlist skyrocketed from about 5,000 to 75,000 people eager to try it. This small-scale experiment validated the startup's idea without writing a single line of new code. If it didn't work, and it was a totally failure, then it would have been a quick pivot. A lesson, not a loss.

The same goes for Google's famous "41 shades of blue" test in which they tried tiny color variations in their links to see which one performed best. They ran A/B tests with dozens of blue variations, each shown to a small percentage of users. This was a trivial change to the naked eye, but the results were profound. Google discovered that one slightly different hue of blue attracted more clicks than the others. Implementing that optimal shade of blue across their interfaces had a massive payoff, as it generated an estimated $200 million in additional annual ad revenue.[4] In other words, a tiny tweak – changing a color by a few hex values – led to a huge business impact. Conversely, if it didn't work, no harm done. It was just one micro-adjustment in a sea of thousands. That's the safety net of small steps: they're low risk, high learning, and endlessly adaptable.

For Google and Dropbox, these small steps led to massive payoff, but let's look at couple examples where they didn't work. For example, Instagram started as Burbn, a bloated app with check-ins, photos, and gamified features, but it seemed that users only cared about the photo sharing. So the founders stripped away everything else. That one small course correction transformed the product into what we now know as Instagram. It was a micro-pivot, based on behavior, not ego. They didn't throw out the whole product they simply trimmed the noise. Small product testing revealed the core value. They adjusted early, rather than waiting too long and failing with a bloated launch.

Basecamp's founders constantly preach simplicity. They've made hundreds of small tweaks to their product, and often reversed them just as quickly. One time, they introduced a new feature, only to realize users found it confusing. Instead of pushing forward, they quietly rolled it back and wrote a blog post about what they learned. David Heinemeier Hansson recalls that simply moving a tab to another page triggered enough confusion and frustration that the team backed it out.[5] That's why they treat product changes as small bets: easy to try, easy to reverse, and rich in learning. They view product development as a series of

---

4. Source: https://www.theguardian.com/technology/2014/feb/05/why-google-engineers-designers?utm_source=chatgpt.com

5 Source: https://businessofsoftware.org/talks/david-heinemeier-hansson-rewrite-basecamp-business-of-software-conference-video-dhh-bos2015/

"small bets," which gives them the freedom to experiment and recover fast if the step/bet isn't a winning one.

When you build through small, intentional steps, you don't just reduce the cost of failure but you build confidence in it. You learn to fail without fear, pivot without shame, and turn every misstep into forward motion. As a result, you don't just get better at succeeding. You get better at failing in ways that move you forward.

The 3 Types of Micro-Actions That Lead to Big Growth

Not all micro-actions are created equal. Some simply check boxes. Others build empires. Over the years, I've found that the most high-leverage micro-actions fall into three core categories. When you use them together, they create momentum that becomes unstoppable. Let's break them down.

1. Process-Driven Micro-Actions
The Daily Systems That Create Success

It's easy to become fixated on the big goal. Most people do. They map out timelines, dream up milestones, and wait for motivation to carry them across the finish line. But those who scale understand that goals alone aren't enough. What gets you there are your daily systems.

A system is what happens when action becomes automatic. It's the structure that keeps you moving when inspiration fades, when things get hard, or when you simply don't feel like showing up. Scaling up requires rhythm and repetition. The kind of consistency that isn't always exciting, but is always effective.

You can set all the ambitious targets in the world, but without a process to support them, they remain out of reach. James Clear said it best in *Atomic Habits*: **"You do not rise to the level of your goals. You fall to the level of your systems."** A goal gives you direction, but a system gives you traction.

Maybe your goal is to grow your business, land more clients, or become known in your industry. You don't need a massive breakthrough to make that happen. You need one small action, done every day, that builds toward that future. One connection made. One pitch sent. One promise kept to yourself.

Process-driven micro-actions are the foundation of sustainable growth because they shift success from something you chase to something you practice. The more you practice, the more natural it becomes. That's when scaling stops feeling like a battle and starts to feel like a rhythm you can trust.

Reflection Questions

- What's one small action I can repeat daily that would support my biggest goal right now?

- Where am I relying too heavily on motivation instead of building a reliable system?

- What part of my current routine is quietly holding me back—and what tiny shift could change that?

- Am I prioritizing consistency, or chasing intensity and burning out?

2. Opportunity-Based Micro-Actions
Creating Big Breakthroughs from Small Moves

Opportunity doesn't always knock the way we expect it to. It rarely comes dressed like a breakthrough. More often, it shows up quietly—hidden inside an invitation to speak at a small event, a late-night idea you almost ignore, or a conversation that seems insignificant until it changes everything.

People often wait for something big to signal that it's time to act. They hold out for clarity, for perfect conditions, for the moment that feels worthy of risk. But those who scale understand that the most important opportunities rarely arrive with fanfare. They show up as something small. The only way to recognize them is to keep showing up yourself. Lift every little stone to see where it might lead.

One small, intentional action at a time. A thoughtful email. A decision to overdeliver. A willingness to be present when it would be easier to check out. These are the micro-actions that open doors. Not always immediately, but consistently, quietly, and often unexpectedly.

What looks like a small task—one more Zoom call, one post no one responds to, one moment of excellence that goes unacknowledged—might be the very thing that leads to your next breakthrough. But you don't get to know that in advance. You just have to trust that small effort still matters, even when no one's watching.

That's how opportunity works. It grows in the margins. It builds when you keep saying yes to things that feel a little too small to matter—until one day, they do.

Reflection Questions

- Have I been overlooking any small opportunities because they didn't look like a "big deal"?

- When was the last time I chose to overdeliver, even when no one asked me to?

- What small task or connection am I tempted to dismiss—but could lead somewhere if I stayed present with it?

- If I treated today like it mattered, what would I do differently?

3. Mindset-Based Micro-Actions
The Invisible Shifts That Change Everything

Some of the most important actions you'll ever take won't be visible to anyone else, not even you, at first. They happen inside. Quietly. Subtly. Almost like a breath you didn't know you were holding. A shift in thought. A soft recalibration. A moment where you stop spiraling in doubt and decide to believe something different, even if just for a day.

This is the power of mindset-based micro-actions. They don't show up on a checklist. You can't track them on a spreadsheet. But they shape everything about how you show up in the world. They're the inner work behind the outer results.

Transformation happens gradually, in all the tiny decisions to believe a little more in yourself, to try again when it didn't work the first time, to act from vision instead of fear. It's in choosing to ask, "What if this works?" instead of "What if I fail?" even once. Then again. And again.

These invisible shifts become anchors. They hold you steady in the hard seasons. They give you courage when the stakes get higher. Over time, they rewire the way you think, choose, and lead.

Reflection Questions

- What's one limiting belief I keep returning to—and what might be possible if I let it go?
- When was the last time I chose courage over certainty?
- What would the next-level version of me believe about today's challenges?
- Can I give myself permission to act, even if I don't feel ready?

The Art of Making It Small Enough to Succeed

One of the biggest mistakes people make with small steps is assuming they're small when they're actually not. A goal like "write my book" turns into "write 2,000 words a day," which might sound manageable at first…until it isn't. A business owner sets the goal of "reach out to 10 leads every morning," then burns out by Thursday. The problem isn't the ambition. It's the scale.

Small steps only work if they're truly small. So small that they feel almost effortless. So small that they don't trigger resistance. So small that your nervous system barely flinches when you begin. This allows you to keep going indefinitely, to build your muscle, and gradually increase.

That's the art of a real micro-action. And it takes practice to get right.

Start by looking at the thing you want to achieve. Then ask yourself: What's the first obvious action I'd need to take? Now take that, and cut it in half. Then cut it in half again. That's the territory you're aiming for. Small enough to feel easy, doable, almost frictionless.

When the action is that small, something powerful happens: you complete it. That completion triggers a subtle but important reward, both consciously and subconsciously. You feel a win. A sense of momentum. That small win starts to feel good, so you come back to it. It becomes something you don't have to force. Something you can enjoy doing every day. Because every day, you succeed, and eventually, it becomes fun.

If your goal is to get in shape, your micro-action might not be "go to the gym." It might be "put on your sneakers and walk around the block." If you want to write a book, your micro-action isn't "write a chapter." It might be "open the document and write one paragraph." If you're trying to get visible in your industry, maybe it's not "post a reel every day." Maybe it's just "comment thoughtfully on one person's content."

How small your action needs to be depends on you, and you alone. No one else can decide that for you. The only rule is this: it has to be small enough to create a sense of success. Something so easy, so doable, that you enjoy doing it. That's how you build consistency. Once it starts to feel boring or effortless? That's your cue to gently add more, and just enough that it's challenging fun, but not defeat.

The goal isn't to impress anyone. The goal is to begin and remain consistent. When that beginning feels safe, repeatable, and low-friction, you'll do it again tomorrow. And the next day. And the one after that. That's how momentum is born, and that's how you Scale Up.

"If it feels so small it's almost laughable… you're doing it right. Progress isn't always thrilling. At first, it's quiet. Boring. Repetitive. And then suddenly — it's who you are."

Looking Ahead

You now understand the power of micro-actions—and how they build real, sustainable momentum. But momentum without discipline burns out. Energy without systems breaks down, and ambition without structure eventually collapses. That's why the next building block is essential.

In the next chapter, we'll explore **Disciplined Execution**—and how to build the systems, routines, and habits that make your success inevitable. Let's keep building.

Checklist

Building Block - 4 Small Steps

The Micro-Actions That Drive Big Growth

Quick Win Checklist:

- ✓ Choose one big goal and break it into 5–7 small, measurable steps.
- ✓ Identify the single smallest action you can take today to move that goal forward.
- ✓ Create a recurring 10-minute "micro-action" time block in your calendar for the next two weeks.
- ✓ Track your progress daily — focus on consistency, not perfection.
- ✓ Celebrate one small win this week, no matter how minor it seems.

Shareable Content:

Your Turn:

Look at one area of your life or business you want to scale — and break it down until the next step feels almost laughably small. Then do it. Not once, but every day this week.

Track how you feel. Track what shifts. Watch how momentum builds, not from effort, but from consistency.

Want to go deeper? Share your micro-action publicly and tag it with #ScaleUpBlueprint to inspire others to do the same.

Social Media Ready:

"Don't wait for motivation. Build a system. That's how success becomes sustainable." #ScaleUpBlueprint #MicroActions

"If your next step doesn't feel small enough to fail at, it's probably too big." #SmallStepsBigGrowth #ScaleUpBlueprint

"The people who scale aren't more talented. They just do the small things more consistently." #ScaleUpBlueprint #DailyMomentum

"Small wins stack. Quiet effort compounds. That's the real blueprint for growth." #ScaleUpBlueprint #UnstoppableGrowth

Chapter 8

Building Block #5 – Discipline: The Power of Discipline & Consistency

It's not what you do once that scales you. It's what you repeat when no one's clapping.

We often associate discipline with high performers, the 5 a.m. club, color-coded calendars, militant routines, and so on. But real discipline isn't rooted in pressure or perfection or militant ways. It's rooted in the quiet decision to stay aligned, especially when no one else understands your choice. It's saying *yes* to what serves your long game, and saying *no* to what doesn't. It's making small consistent choices over and over again. That's why **Building Block #5 in the Scale Up Blueprint™ is The Power of Discipline & Consistency**. Brilliance can spark something amazing, but discipline is what sustains it.

Why Discipline Is Often the Missing Link

Scaling doesn't happen because of one strength; it happens when multiple strengths work together. This includes your vision, mindset, support, small steps, and more. Among all these, discipline is often where the system breaks down. People start strong, but they don't stay the course. They rely on motivation, which fades. They chase intensity, and crash. They expect overnight or fast results, and give up too soon.

Without discipline, even the most brilliant plans collapse because of inconsistency.

This is where Building Block #5 comes in. Not to carry the whole system, but to sustain it. Discipline is built in the quiet decision to keep aligning your actions with your vision, even when no one's watching or understands what you are doing. This building block keeps everything else moving.

When Discipline Means Letting Go

While there are three Identity Shifts that are crucial to having a disciplined mind, I want to share with you personal example of one that addresses The Identity Shift #1 – Becoming Someone Who Doesn't Betray Their Own Vision.

This is one of the most difficult shifts to do because, often, it means that your support system building block is shaken up. As we know, when we shake up one building block, we risk losing ground on all others. So this shift has to be executed in a way that it brings you wins at the end without crumbling everything else.

Not long ago, for me it looked like everything was finally coming together. My work was flourishing. My body was strong. I was building a life that felt expansive and deeply aligned. I have been used to growing and constantly scaling up, so being in that groove feels good to me. It's fun, exciting, and often hard, but most of all-it's rewarding. That mode allows me to build the life I want and become the best version of myself.

I was in a relationship with someone I cared for deeply. but underneath that surface, something wasn't right. The relationship wasn't toxic. It wasn't dramatic. It wasn't a cautionary tale. It just… didn't fit. We loved each other, yes. But it seemed that love alone wasn't enough.

I wrestled for a long time trying to answer the question "why?" Why was I feeling like this? Why was I feeling like something was missing? In my search, I realized that being with this person meant settling. Staying the same, and not constantly growing and scaling up. That's not who I am as a person, nor is it how I want to live my life. As a result, our visions for the future were misaligned. The way we communicated, the pace we moved through life, the energy we brought to each other-it all slowly started to chip away at the version of me I had worked so hard to become. My internal systems, my inner sonar, was rebelling. I wasn't living my truth anymore. I was no longer aligned, and this wasn't working.

I ignored it at first, because it's so easy to justify staying things like: "No one's perfect." "It's not that bad." "Maybe if I just work harder at this…" But deep down, I knew. This relationship was pulling me out of alignment with myself. The longer I stayed, the more it was costing me, not in blowups or betrayals, but in quiet, invisible ways. My energy. My clarity. My ability to show up fully. Would I possibly arrive at the end of my life with massive regrets? So I made a decision to walk away.

It's important to remember that discipline isn't always forward motion. Sometimes it's the leadership to pause. To restrain. To release. To let go. To regroup. Sometimes, it's about walking away from something that almost works, because you know it won't sustain the version of you you're becoming. In my case, leaving wasn't easy, but it was necessary. In that choice, I learned one of the most difficult and important lessons of my life. Discipline isn't just about showing up. It's about not abandoning yourself when it's easier to abandon your vision.

This type of Identity Shift is crucial to note. It's ever so subtle and no one is talking about it. If your internal self and who you are is not consistent with the outer environment and who you are showing up as, your ability to show up consistently will be jeopardize and almost impossible. If you believe deep down that you want to be a CEO or an entrepreneur, yet your environment is forcing you to do something else, you will not be able to stay consistent with that "something else." Your deep belief, your lack of care, your betrayal of yourself will not allow you. This is why you have to be aligned and sometimes choose to leave the environment, people, organizations, jobs, that don't align with your goals.

As I mentioned, this is particularly difficult because leaving behind things that are not aligned with you sometimes means leaving behind part of your support system. For me, it wasn't just a relationship I was leaving, I was also leaving my best friend. I had to explain to my family and close friends why I was doing this seemingly wrong and unsettling thing. It shook part of my most imprint building block, the foundation - Support System. But, I have aligned myself with exceptional people and my support system is unwavering. They always want what's best for me. They were all able to see the long-term value and benefit of this decisions and step into a supportive role. I hope you can see how these building blocks are crucial and how they truly build on each other, working together in unison to keep you scaling up with confidence.

"Employees who feel authentic at work are significantly more engaged, more consistent, and less likely to burn out.

Because you can't force discipline in a life that contradicts who you are. When identity aligns with environment, consistency follows."

— Based on research from the
Journal of Applied Psychology

Why Small Steps Make Discipline Possible

Before we dive into the shifts that make discipline sustainable, we have recognize the importance of the previous building block - Small Steps.

The smaller the step, the easier it is to stay consistent. We often think discipline means pushing ourselves harder. But in reality, discipline is about removing friction and difficulty so staying consistent is easy. We want to make it easy to show up, again and again. That's why Building Block #4—The Power of Small Steps—is so essential. When your steps are too big it becomes more difficult to remain consistent, motivation wears off, it's no longer satisfying or fun, and it becomes more and more difficult to keep up. But when when your steps are small and repeatable, your momentum builds. It's fun, and discipline becomes a natural progress in scaling up.

For me, I could leave that relationship not because I was brave every day and had to face major obstacles. It was because I made one honest decision at a time, small, simple decision that got me to the next small decision. One day, I said no to a weekend trip, not because I didn't care, but because I knew I needed that time to be with myself. I didn't make it a fight. I just chose me, gently. Little by little. This allowed me to stay aligned with my long game. I chose tiny, consistent actions that honored who I was becoming.

Remember that discipline doesn't ask for grand gestures; it asks for repeatable ones. When your steps are small, you stay in motion. When you stay in motion, you scale. It's that simple.

The 3 Identity Shifts That Lead to Unstoppable Success

These aren't hacks or habits. Rather, they're deep internal shifts that change the way you move through the world. Discipline isn't simply a behavior change, it's a *becoming*. A quiet agreement between who you are and who you're committed to be.

1. The Identity Shift – 1 - Becoming Someone Who Doesn't Betray Their Own Vision

If you see yourself as inconsistent, you'll act inconsistently. If you see yourself as someone who compromises their values to make others comfortable, you'll keep doing that, no matter how ambitious your goals are. But once you decide to become someone who honors themselves, their vision, and their journey, then everything changes. You start showing up differently. You say no faster. You stay the course longer. Consistency can't survive misalignment.

If the person you're trying to be on the outside contradicts who you are on the inside, eventually something will break. You can't force discipline in a life that doesn't reflect your truth. Maybe deep down, you know you're meant to lead, build, and create something of your own. But, if you're stuck in a job, a role, or a relationship that asks you to shrink, settle, or stay silent, your consistency will begin to crumble. Not because you're lazy or lack discipline, but because your soul will always resist betrayal. This is why your identity shift matters so much. You have to become the kind of person who refuses to stay anywhere you don't belong so you can start showing up fully where you do.

This concept isn't just personal, it's proven. Research across industries and organizations consistently shows that identity alignment isn't a soft skill. It's a performance multiplier. A major study published in the Journal of Applied Psychology found that employees who feel they can be authentic at work experience higher engagement, stronger job performance, and significantly lower burnout. In fact, according to Gallup, employees who strongly agree with the statement *"I have the opportunity to do what I do best every day"* are 6 times more likely to be engaged, 3 times more likely to report excellent quality of life, and 15% less likely to quit. These metrics reflect the cost of misalignment, disengagement, inconsistency, and quiet quitting.

Nowhere is the power of alignment more visible than at Patagonia, one of the most admired, mission-driven companies in the world. Their hiring process is intentionally values based. They don't just look for skill sets; they look for people who are already living their (Patagonia's) mission.

The results are extraordinary. In retail, where annual turnover can exceed 65%, Patagonia's employee turnover hovers around 4%. Not because their work is easy, but because their people believe in it. It's aligned with their values, so it's fun and easy to keep showing up.

Employees are encouraged to surf during lunch breaks, attend climate rallies, or take time off to volunteer for causes that matter to them. Their outer roles don't contradict their inner identity. They reflect it. That's why their consistency isn't forced. When who you are and what you do are aligned, you don't need to summon discipline every day. You just show up, because it feels like truth. This provides perpetual commitment and loyalty. Conversely, when those two are in conflict, no amount of self-control will carry you long term. For a period, yes. But long term, no.

That's the power of the identity shift. It frees you to be consistent, not because you're forcing it, but because you've stopped fighting yourself.

2. The Process Shift 2 – Loving the Act, Not Just the Outcome

Discipline becomes unbearable only when it's tied to the result. This is because results don't arrive on schedule. They stall. They plateau. They show up late. If your consistency is only anchored in the payoff, you'll quit long before it ever comes. That's why the real shift, the one that makes discipline sustainable, is falling in love with the process itself. Not just tolerating it or pushing through it, but learning to value the act of showing up, even when the reward is nowhere in sight. Showing up becomes the reward.

At first, that might sound unrealistic. How do you love something that feels repetitive or slow or uncertain?
The answer is simple: you don't wait for the process to become pleasurable, you bring meaning to it. If you infuse meaning to anything you do, it will become more fun. With meaning, this mundane thing has a purpose and a meaning. Anything I do, I do it with meaning, and you need to do the same. Regardless of what you do, or how small it is assign it, a powerful meaning that will fill you up.

For example, if you are trying to work out and stay disciplined about exercising every day, it is important to assign meaning to those workouts. The meaning could be staying healthy to be there for your children. You are aware, each time you go to the gym, your children are watching you and you are modeling behavior for them - you are modeling self-care, consistency, priority, and health, among many other things. Now when you get up and perhaps don't feel so motivated to go to the gym, you can reach for that meaning to give you the nudge you need. Same applies to your work - regardless if you are a leader you job is to fall in love with the process and make that fun. Discipline will be a result you won't have to worry about.

At IDEO, one of the world's most innovative companies, their teams aren't taught to obsess over final outcomes. They're taught to fall in love with iterations, prototyping, and learning. They treat the creative process itself as a success, even when the first five versions fail. That mindset has fueled some of the most consistent breakthroughs in global product design.

It's the same in our personal lives. When we start measuring effort instead of outcome—when we ask "Did I show up today?" instead of "Did I win today?"—something begins to shift.

That shift is backed by research. A 2021 Harvard Business Review study found that people who tracked and celebrated progress in the process, not just the result, were 46% more likely to sustain their goals long term. Gallup has shown that employees who describe their daily work as "personally meaningful" are 4.6 times more engaged and 57% more productive than those who only chase results.

Because joy matters, and meaning matters. Those two things, joy and meaning, aren't found at the finish line, they're built into the process itself.

Discipline becomes easier when the work feels like something more than a chore. This happens when it becomes a ritual, and a moment of self-respect. It is a reflection of who you are and what you care about. Even in fitness, research shows that people who find pleasure in the act of moving, whether it's walking outside, dancing, or lifting weights, are twice as likely to stay consistent as those who are focused solely on metrics like weight loss or time.

When you fall in love with the practice, not for what it gets you, but for how it honors you, you stop dragging yourself through life. You start building momentum no one can take away from you.

This shift isn't loud. It's not dramatic. But it's the difference between discipline that burns you out, and discipline that carries you forward. Fall in love with the doing. Not because it's easy, but because it's the truest expression of the life you're choosing to build.

"People who celebrate the process—not just the results—are 46% more likely to sustain their goals long term. Discipline doesn't require force. It requires meaning. Build a practice you respect, and the consistency will come."
— *Harvard Business Review, 2021*

3. The Long Game Shift - 3 – Making Peace with Slow

We live in a world that rewards urgency. Get there faster. Grow quicker. Scale yesterday. We're conditioned to crave instant confirmation that we're on the right path. Regardless if it's the deal closing, the weight dropping, the person texting back. Whatever it is, we want it now. Heck, I am guilty of buying Amazon items solely because they will arrive today at my house instead of tomorrow. Technology makes it so easy for us to get wrapped up into instant gratification.

Regardless of how we feel, most things that matter take longer than we want them to. They often happen on a timeline different than what we had in mind, because we can not control the universe, despite how much we try.

Progress, real progress, rarely happens on cue. Discipline breaks down when our expectations aren't built for the wait. The people who stay the course are the ones who've made peace with the fact that some seeds take time to bloom. And that's okay. They've learned how to keep showing up while the results are still invisible.

I learned this lesson on many occasions in my personal life. Once it was during that season of walking away from the relationship I once hoped would last. The decision to leave was hard, but the grief afterward was even harder. The silence. The doubt. The ache of wondering whether I'd made the right call or not. And yet, staying would have cost more than leaving. The hardest part is that the clarity of my situation (or any situation), doesn't always arrive immediately. Often it takes its time. Eventually, my grief softened. The clarity deepened. The peace became something I could finally trust. Knowing how to delay your gratification for long-term success is essential in maintaining consistency, discipline, and scaling up.

This kind of long-range thinking isn't just helpful, it's also foundational. Research published in the Journal of Personality and Social Psychology followed children into adulthood and found that those with stronger future orientation and the ability to regulate behavior over time were significantly more likely to succeed in education, health, and professional life. The key wasn't just patience—it was the belief that their actions now would meaningfully shape their future.[6] We see this in leadership, too. According to a 2023 Harvard Business Review report, companies that prioritize long-term strategy over short-term profits see 47% higher revenue growth and are 81% more likely to deliver sustained innovation.

Amazon is a classic example of this. For over a decade, Jeff Bezos told shareholders he wasn't optimizing for quarterly profits. He was building infrastructure for long-term dominance. At the time, he was met with laughter and doubt. But by 2020, that "slow game" strategy turned Amazon into one of the most valuable companies in the world. Similarly, at Costco, CEO Jim Sinegal famously said, "If you want me to turn in a good quarter, I can do it, but I'm not going to destroy the company in the process." Today, Costco outperforms most of its competitors because it moves slow and steady with integrity over extended periods of time.

---

6. Source: Mischel, Shoda, & Peake (1990)

The most successful leaders I've met, and the ones I've admired from afar, scale because they stay and think in terms of long-term success. In business, in healing, in relationships, it's the long game that holds the gold. You stop expecting it to happen overnight. You stop needing it to look a certain way by a certain date. You start respecting the rhythm of real growth. When you stop rushing the process, you finally become the person capable of sustaining what's coming.

"Companies that prioritize long-term strategy over short-term gains grow 47% faster and innovate 81% more consistently.

The same is true for people. Fast fades. But discipline—that stays."
— *Harvard Business Review, 2023*

Discipline Is the Infrastructure of Greatness

Anyone can make a bold move. Anyone can post a win, light up a room, or start something with fire. But that's not what builds anything that lasts. If you want to scale, then you have to find a way to last and play a long-term game utilizing discipline as one of your core tools. You have to find a way to stay with your craft, to stay with your values, to stay with your true self, especially when it's hard. To keep showing up long after it stops being exciting. You don't need a finish line or applause to keep moving or stay consistent. You understand that momentum isn't created in moments of motivation; instead, it is created in the quiet. In the rhythm and repetition.

Discipline doesn't look like a breakthrough. It looks like a decision, made again and again in private until the results become public. Discipline is about being anchored. This is how the dream becomes real. This is how the vision becomes structure. This is how the system builds itself, one steady choice at a time. Discipline is what makes success sustainable. Sustainability is what turns a spark into a legacy.

Reflection Questions

Where are you staying loyal to something that no longer aligns with your long game?

Where could your life be in a year if you simply stayed the course, gently and consistently?

Where have you been relying on motivation instead of building systems?

What identity do you need to adopt to act with greater consistency?

What would change if you stopped chasing fast results and started mastering the long game?

Looking Ahead

Discipline builds momentum. But even the strongest momentum can be interrupted, by loss, by failure, by moments that blindside you and leave you breathless. When the rhythm breaks, when the structure shakes, it's not discipline that carries you forward. It's tenacity.

In the next chapter, we'll explore what it means to keep going when everything in you wants to stop. To hold the thread when it feels like it's slipping through your fingers. To rebuild your momentum from the ground up—and rise, even when the world tells you it's too late.

Let's keep building.

Checklist

Building Block - 5 Discipline

The Power of Discipline & Consistency

Quick Win Checklist:

- ✓ Choose one habit that, if done daily, will create long-term impact — and commit to it for 30 days.
- ✓ Set a specific time each day to work on your most important task — and protect it fiercely.
- ✓ Create an accountability system (partner, app, or checklist) to track your discipline.
- ✓ Remove one distraction that consistently pulls you away from your work.
- ✓ Reward yourself at the end of the week for following through on your commitments.

Shareable Content:

Your Turn:

You don't need to be more intense. You need to be more consistent. And the best way to become consistent is to build a life that aligns with who you truly are.

This week, ask yourself:
- Where am I still waiting for motivation instead of building systems?
- What part of my process needs more joy, meaning, or ritual?
- Where in my life am I still chasing speed instead of trusting the long game?
- What would it look like to scale—not through pressure—but through quiet, steady discipline?

Share your insights or small wins using **#ScaleUpBlueprint**
We'd love to hear how you're integrating this building block into your life or business.

Social Media Ready:

Discipline is what makes success sustainable. Not pressure. Not perfection. Not a big burst of energy. Just small choices, made consistently, in alignment with who you really are. #ScaleUpBlueprint

You can't be consistent in a life that betrays who you are.
Authenticity isn't optional—it's structural. When your identity aligns with your path, discipline becomes second nature. #Leadership #ScaleUpBlueprint

Motivation is loud. Discipline is quiet. One fades. The other builds empires. #Discipline #ScaleUpBlueprint

Chapter 9

Building Block #6 - Tenacity: Resilience, Grit & Tenacity in the Scaling Process or Tenacity & Overcoming Setbacks

It's not that they didn't face setbacks. It's that they refused to stop at them.

Success doesn't go to the smartest, the luckiest, or the most talented. It goes to the ones who refuse to quit. Every leader, entrepreneur, visionary, and game-changing company has faced a moment when it would have been easier to stop, accept the loss, and walk away. Some certainly did. But the ones who scaled and became unstoppable didn't quit. They kept going, not because it was easy, but because they were committed to something bigger than the discomfort they were facing. They understood that setbacks aren't the end of the road; they're part of the road. That's why Building Block #6 of the Scale Up Blueprint™ is **Resilience, Grit & Tenacity**.

Everyone loves a comeback story.

But no one wants to live one.

No one wants to wake up every day in pain. Or walk into another meeting pretending everything's fine when inside, you're unraveling. No one wants to keep building when the scaffolding inside you feels like it's cracking. No one wants to fall.

But people who scale the highest aren't the ones who never fall. They're the ones who fall, but decide to get up. Not once, not twice, but every time, over and over again. Even when they don't know what they're getting up for anymore. That's what tenacity is. Tenacity, resilience, and grit aren't some grand acts of courage, they are subtle choices to stay even when everything in you wants to run.

I know that feeling, because I built my first company while carrying the full weight of unprocessed trauma and dealing with a severe case of PTSD. I was running a successful IT business with a growing team, award-winning clients, and measurable results. From the outside, it looked like I had everything together. In some ways, I did. I was meeting deadlines, signing contracts, and speaking at conferences.

But what no one saw were the flashbacks. The sleepless nights. The night terrors. The fear that swallowed me whole. The meetings I took after crying in the bathroom. The moments when a certain sound or image sent me spiraling, right back to a war zone I had left years ago. That's the part no one tells you about scaling. When you decide to scale up and grow, you don't get to leave your humanity at the door. It comes with you, all of your fears and beliefs and all of your unprocessed trauma. As you scale, all of you is coming along for the ride.

There were days I wanted to burn the whole thing down. Not because I didn't love what I was doing, but because I couldn't keep carrying the weight and smiling on cue. The pressure of leading a team while still learning how to regulate my nervous system felt unbearable. The pressure of having to get up on stage and motivate people while inside of me I was crumbling.

I remember one keynote in particular. I was in Las Vegas speaking to a Fortune 100 organization. I've always battled survivors guilt, and, as a result, I tend to constantly do things that "justify" my existence. Any chance I have to help others, especially at scale, I take it. Being a keynote speaker allows me to feel that my survival was worth it. That universe sparing my life was a good thing, because I am doing good things with it. I get to touch many lives at once and inspire them to live better, hope more, and become a better version of themselves.

Feeling like I am doing good is the main reason for my speaking, my books, and everything I do. At this particular event were more than five thousand attendees. It was held on a large stage in a fantastic Las Vegas hotel. Everything felt like a dream, especially for a little girl from Bosnia with a turbulent past. Who could have imagined that I would grow up to do this? I flew first class, checked into a hotel I'd only seen in movies, and stood on a stage before thousands of people. It felt surreal.

I got to a beautiful suite overlooking the strip with glass from floor to ceiling. The view was stunning. I was living the dream. But the flip side of that was — my fear of flying was exacerbated by my severe PTSD symptoms. I was battling hours-long panic attacks. To make matters worse, the vacuum system that I was using to keep my prosthetic leg on failed, and I was in severe physical pain. Once I got to hotel and was able to remove my prosthetic leg, I realized that my residual limb was covered with bloody blisters, dozens of them covering almost every inch of my skin. After realizing the extent of the damage, I stayed in bed and couldn't enjoy Las Vegas or even go out to dinner. But the worse was yet to come.

The last thing I wanted to do was slide my prosthetic leg onto these blistered and open wounds, let alone put pressure on it when I walked. But, my speech was tomorrow morning, and that meant I would be walking most of the day. It started with a sound check early in the morning. Then, in a couple hours, I had to walk on stage for at least an hour. After my speech would be the usual after-speech meet and greet. And once I put my leg on in the morning, it was best to keep it on without removing it until the day was done. Taking it on and off would rip open old wounds while creating new ones.

Battling physical pain and severe symptoms from my PTSD, like panic attacks and night terrors, made me want to throw in the towel and be done. It made me feel like a fraud, like I had no business standing in front of people trying to inspire hope and positivity. But I didn't throw in the towel. I stayed. I showed up. Not because it was easy or I was especially brave or strong, but because I knew the mission was bigger than the storm I was weathering. I knew that the moment I stepped on that stage, I would see the reason why. I knew that the moment I got off of that stage and people started coming up to me to tell me how my speech changed their life and now they feel like they could handle the crises in their life, it would be worth it.

And it was true. When I stepped on that stage, looking at thousands of attendees listening to me so intently you could hear a pin drop, I forgot about my pain. I forgot about panic attacks. I forgot about PTSD. All I could see was the difference I was making in touching these people's lives. The pain and PTSD became nothing more than a small price to pay for a greater goal and outcome.

Tenacity, I learned, is not about ignoring your pain. It's about building anyway. It is about recognizing the pain, acknowledging the pain, and making room for it. It means sitting with the pain. It means choosing to keep moving forward because the pain is temporary and the ultimate outcome is far greater. That version of me who showed up every day to run my business or speak on stages was doing the hardest work of all. That version of me was healing while building. And that version of me is the reason I am able to continue scaling up despite any obstacles I face.

That combination of scaling while healing exists in you too. This is the version of you that is resilient, tenacious, and more powerful than you know. It is able to conquer anything. It's your job and responsibly to wake up that version of yourself. It's time to rise, not in spite of the pain, but with it.

Why Most People and Businesses Don't Make It

Most people start strong. Most companies launch with excitement. Most leaders begin with vision and drive. But very few keep going when the excitement fades, the path gets hard, and the results don't come fast enough. They let one failure define them. They take rejection as a sign to quit. They assume resistance means they were never meant to succeed. And because of that, they stop—just inches from their breakthrough. They never realize how close they were. How many times the finish line was around the next corner. How much further they could have gone if they'd just stayed in the game. That's what separates those who scale from those who stall. Success is never about the absence of failure. It's about the refusal to let failure be the final chapter.

"Tenacity isn't loud. It's the quiet decision to keep showing up—even when your wounds are still healing."

The Three Tenacity Shifts That Turn Setbacks into Success

There's a reason tenacity is often misunderstood. Most people confuse it with grit-your-teeth endurance or working 18-hour days. But true tenacity is quieter than that. It is more strategic. It's not about burning out. It's about *not backing down.* That tenacity lives in three powerful mindset shifts that separate those who scale from those who stall.

1. From Discomfort-Avoidant to Resilience-Built

Most people avoid discomfort because they think it means something's wrong, but discomfort is the weight room of growth. It's where the resilience muscle gets built. Every time you keep going through difficulty, you build mental and emotional strength. You learn that pain doesn't have to be permanent. You come to understand that failure doesn't mean you're finished. The stronger your resilience muscle, the easier it is to face the next challenge. You know you've done hard things before. Discomfort isn't the sign to stop. It's the signal you're growing.

Studies led by the American Psychological Association and cited by the National Academies reveal that leaders who foster emotional resilience—not just in themselves but across their teams—achieve significantly stronger outcomes during crises. For example:

- Teams with leaders who actively build a supportive workplace climate report that 86% of their employees feel valued and 91% feel motivated in high-pressure environments—compared to just 12% and 38%, respectively, in teams without that support

- Such emotionally resilient workplaces also see far higher participation in wellness efforts, better psychological safety, and sustained performance—underscoring the direct link between leadership resilience and organizational effectiveness

Although the exact figure cited previously (20–30% higher performance) was an estimate based on patterns across multiple studies, these APA-backed data show qualitatively and quantitatively what that performance bump actually looks like in real-world terms: notably improved motivation, engagement, and resilience under stress.

Tenacity vs. Stubbornness

One crucial thing to note is that tenacity is not about pushing through everything at all costs. That's stubbornness and often, ego. Unlike true tenacity and resilience, stubbornness and pride can cost you more than you realize. If you can't tell the difference between the two, you'll either quit too early, or stay too long in something that you should have let go a long time ago.

There are two kinds of pain on the growth path. One is the pain of expansion. It's uncomfortable, stretching, and sometimes even exhausting, but it leads to strength. It teaches you. It shapes you. That pain is worth pushing through. The other is the pain of misalignment. Of clinging to a version of yourself, a goal, or a role that no longer fits. That pain isn't a sign to push harder, it's a signal to pause, reassess, and choose differently.

The only person who can truly see the difference between the two for you, is you - and only you.

It's like working out at the gym with a trainer. There is type of pain and discomfort you feel in your bones and muscles that you know is the good kind of pain. Sometimes, you can feel that pain two days later, but it feels good, because you know you are getting stronger. You are growing and expanding.

And then, there is bad pain. Perhaps it's a sharp sudden pain, and you just know you can't push through that because it will create more damage, or even permanent damage. It will definitely not make you stronger. And so you decide to stop working out. Think about your life like you are in a gym, working out, and YOU have to decide when to push through when to pull back. No one can feel that for you. Even the best trainer in the world can't tell you when enough is enough. They can guess, but only you will know the right answer.

I live with chronic pain every day. That's not a dramatic statement, it's just the truth of my body. Some pain is always there. It doesn't go away. It's part of how I move through the world. And over the years, I've had to learn how to live fully with pain, without letting it consume me.

For example, I love to play tennis. I played tennis even before I learned to run again, and even while walking with painful prosthetics and braces. Playing tennis hurt my legs, and I could barely walk afterward. But I also knew what it gave me. It gave me power, strength, endorphins. It gave me myself. It cleared my mind. It regulated my nervous system. And so, I made it part of my life in a way that served me, not hurt me.

I developed a ritual. The night before tennis, I'd take a long bath, tending to my legs—cleaning wounds, removing scar tissue, preparing them for a beating they were about to endure. I knew what was coming. But I also planned for the aftermath. The two days after tennis was a total rest. Ahead of time I cleared my calendar and stayed home. Watched movies. Let my body recover. Because as much as I respected the push, I respected the pause just as much.

That's the wisdom you need to master. Just because something hurts doesn't mean it's wrong. And just because you can push doesn't mean you always should. I wasn't pushing to prove something or causing permanent damage. I wasn't chasing pain. I was listening to myself. I knew the difference between the pain of expansion and the pain of injury. And I honored both.

That's what tenacity looks like. It's not reckless. It's rhythmic. It's intentional. It's the art of discerning how far to go—and when to stop—so you can keep doing what you love for years to come.

It's the same with scaling a business or your life. Sometimes you push. Sometimes you rest. But the goal is the same: to sustain the joy. To keep going—not just harder, but smarter.

You have to become your own internal coach. You have to be able to differentiate between when to stop and when to push on.

And like everything else, the more you practice, the more fluent you become. You start to notice the difference faster. You know how to adjust. You know when to lean in—and when to let go. The more you walk this path, the more fluent you become in the language of your own discomfort and the faster you'll differentiate between painful growth opportunities that will catapult you versus stubbornness and ego so you can pull back. You start to feel the difference in your gut. One feels like you're growing. The other feels like you're disappearing.

That's the quiet genius of tenacity—it's not just about staying. It's about knowing when to stay, and when to go. When to break through, and when to break free. The more you walk this path, the faster you'll know the difference, and the more gracefully you'll scale.

2. From Failure-Fearing to Feedback-Fueled

We've been taught to see failure as final. We are conditioned to fear and avoid failure at all cost. If you do fail, you are encouraged to mask it or pretend it did't happen. This is all wrong. Failure isn't final. It's only final if you quit. If you learn not to quit, then, for you, failure doesn't exist. The proper way to use failure is simply as information. What didn't work? What can I do differently? What lesson did I just earn?

But people who scale treat failure as data, and every stumble becomes a signal. Every rejection becomes a redirection. Every mistake becomes a message. You learn not to personalize the pain, and instead you extract the pattern. You use that information to keep moving further, better, and faster towards your goal.

Failure often triggers shame. But to scale up, you have to rewire that response. You must shift from shame to strategy. That is the difference between those who keep scaling up and those who emotionally implode after a setback.

Remember Thomas Edison and his response to a question about endless failed attempts? His answer is worth repeating and revisiting. He famously replied: "I have not failed. I've just found 10,000 ways that won't work."

He didn't try to hide or reframe his failed attempts, or sugar coat them to protect his ego. He simply didn't see his attempts as failures; he saw them as 10,000 experiments. Each one gave him new insight. Each one closed the gap between what didn't work and what eventually would. For him, failure didn't exist.

That's what feedback-fueled thinking sounds like. It's clear, calm, and curious. None of this means that Edison didn't get frustrated, question himself, or feel the weight of setbacks. He most likely did - he just decided to keep going one more time. All you have to do is decide to keep going, one more time. Until you get there.

Failure is not what slows most people down, it's how they interpret the failure that decides the outcome. If you see it as a verdict, you will stop. If you see it as information, you will adjust and keep going — one more time.

According to a 2022 study published in the Harvard Business Review, leaders who are trained to reframe failure as feedback are 23% more likely to pursue bold initiatives again, even after a public setback. That mindset doesn't just build success. It builds momentum, stamina, and tenacity. Once you stop seeing failure as something to hide, you stop fearing it altogether. When you're no longer afraid of failing, you're free to try. Free to stretch. Free to scale.

> *"Leaders trained to reframe failure as feedback are 23% more likely to pursue bold initiatives after public setbacks."*
> — *Harvard Business Review, 2022*

That's the real power of feedback. It's not about avoiding mistakes. It's about building faster pathways to growth, because you're actually learning from what didn't work.

So the next time you fall flat, ask yourself this:

- What's the data here?
- What's the upgrade hiding inside the discomfort?
- What could this failure make possible?

Do that often enough, and eventually the setbacks won't even feel like setbacks anymore. They'll feel like blueprints, or the momentum and raw material of your next breakthrough.

3. From Fast Results to Long-Game Mastery

We live in a world obsessed with speed. The highlight reels. The 30-under-30s. The viral launches and overnight millionaires. You scroll for two minutes and start to wonder if you're behind, if your life should have scaled faster, louder, or more visibly by now. It's can be so overwhelming.

It's why we would rather take a pain pill and hide the pain than fix the cause. I admit, that speed is seductive. Often I have been tempted to take shortcuts to my end goal, because sometimes life just feels exhausting. But I never do because I know that, like a pain pill, shortcuts will only hide the real cause that I need to work on. To truly build tenacity and resilience, we have to be willing to put in the time.

People who scale something meaningful, who build companies, movements, and careers that actually last, aren't racing toward visibility and quick fixes. They're taking their time, finding the real cause they need to work on, investing in infrastructure, quietly and consistently, often without recognition for years.

Real Life Example

Brené Brown has become a global voice on vulnerability, courage, and leadership. But before the TED stage, the Netflix special, or the bestselling books, Brené was just a researcher at the University of Houston trying to make sense of human emotion. For years, no one was paying attention to her or her work. She wasn't a media personality. She wasn't writing for applause. She was quietly collecting stories and analyzing shame. Mapping out what made people feel disconnected, and what brought them back to life.

Brené didn't brand herself as a thought leader. She wasn't pitching viral topics. She was doing the actual work, one interview and study at a time. For decades. Even her now-famous TEDx talk on vulnerability was delivered at a small, local event in Houston. She never imagined it would go viral. In fact, after it did, she said if she'd known how many people would see it, she wouldn't have said what she said. She wasn't trying to be seen. She was trying to be real. That's tenacity. Showing up when no one's watching, speaking hard truths, and doing the work even when the world is not listening.

Brené didn't rise because she followed a trending path like many "personal growth experts" that fall just as quickly. She rose because she stayed faithful to the message, even when it felt like no one cared. She stayed in integrity with her work, even when it was emotionally taxing, professionally risky, or flat-out uncomfortable.

That's the thing about tenacity, it doesn't always look like pushing. Sometimes it looks like staying, being curious, honest, and open, when it would be so much easier to shut down. For example, Brené didn't chase relevance but she pursued truth. In doing so, she built something that has lasted. Because tenacity isn't just about endurance, it's also about alignment. It is the courage to keep going when your heart is still in it… but the world hasn't caught up yet.

When I was scaling my company, there were long stretches when it felt like nothing was happening. No press. No big launch. No influx of praise. Just systems being refined. Relationships being deepened. Inner leadership being built one invisible decision at a time. Those months felt small, but they became the backbone of everything that came later. I was building foundation, and it turns out, I wasn't alone.

"Teams with emotionally resilient leaders report 86% of employees feel valued—and 91% stay motivated under pressure. Without that leadership support? Those numbers drop to 12% and 38%."

— American Psychological Association / National Academies Research

According to research from Stanford's Graduate School of Business, the majority of Fortune 500 founders spent 5 to 7 years in near total obscurity before gaining traction. T That's the reality behind most success stories that no one posts about. The book that became a bestseller started with a draft no one saw. The product that changed an industry began with a prototype that failed. The leader who became "an overnight success" has been laying bricks quietly for a decade.

So the next time you are scrolling through overnight success stories or organizations that seem to have sprung up, remember there is a whole story behind that 30-second reel that you are not seeing. Every person who has scaled something extraordinary, whether it's a business, a movement, a mission, or a personal transformation, has done so by continuing when others quit. Tenacity is not a trait. It's a choice. And you can make that choice every single day. You don't have to be the best. You just have to keep going.

Reflection Questions

- Where in your life or business have you given up too early?
- What would it look like to recommit to that goal right now?
- What failure could you reframe as feedback—and use as fuel to try again?

Looking Ahead

Tenacity keeps you in the game. It gives you the power to push through resistance. But staying in the game isn't enough, you also need to track your progress, refine your approach, and sustain momentum over time.

In the next chapter, we'll explore the final building block of the Scale Up Blueprint™—how to measure results, sustain your growth, and ensure that your momentum doesn't just last... it multiplies.

Let's keep building.

Checklist

Building Block - 6 Tenacity

Tenacity & Overcoming Setbacks

Quick Win Checklist:

- ✓ Identify one setback you're currently facing and write down three possible paths forward.
- ✓ Revisit a past challenge and note how you overcame it — use it as proof you can do it again.
- ✓ Set one "non-negotiable" action for this week, no matter what obstacles appear.
- ✓ Replace one self-defeating thought with a solution-oriented one.
- ✓ Share your story of overcoming a challenge with someone who might benefit from it.

Shareable Content:

Your Turn:

Tenacity isn't a trait. It's a choice. And it's made in the smallest moments—the day you show up anyway, the moment you try again, the second you decide not to give up. Think of a moment recently where you felt the urge to stop. Where quitting felt easier than continuing. Where it felt like nothing was working.

Now pause and ask yourself:

- What deeper outcome is worth fighting for?
- What version of you is waiting on the other side of this challenge?
- What would it look like to stay in the game—just one more round?

Write down your answer. Say it out loud. Then take one small step. That's all it takes to activate your tenacity.

Share your story using #ScaleUpBlueprint—you never know who you'll inspire to keep going.

Social Media Ready:

Most people quit inches from their breakthrough. They mistake resistance for a "no," when it's really a test. Keep going. The success you're chasing is still chasing you. #ScaleUpBlueprint #Tenacity

Every setback holds a strategy. Every failure hides a reframe.
Every rejection is redirection. You're not stuck. You're just one interpretation away from momentum. #GrowthMindset #ScaleUpBlueprint

"I didn't fail. I just found 10,000 ways that didn't work." – Thomas Edison
That's not optimism. That's tenacity. When failure becomes feedback, the path becomes clear. #Leadership #Tenacity #ScaleUpBlueprint

---

Chapter 10

Building Block #7 – Results: Measuring Results & Sustaining Momentum

What gets measured gets improved. What gets celebrated gets repeated.

Scaling up isn't just about big beginnings or bold decisions. It's also about staying in motion when the adrenaline fades. It's a rhythm you have to learn how to protect, nurture, and sustain.

Far too frequently leaders, organizations, people will give up because they simply can't see how far they've come. They lose the thread of progress. The days blur together. The wins go unnoticed. They burn out, because they never paused long enough to realize they were already moving forward and winning. And that's the danger. You can be growing and still feel stuck. You can be making real progress and not even know it because you're not measuring it. You're in the middle of your own story, so close to it that you forget that you're miles from where you started.

That's why Building Block #7 of the Scale Up Blueprint™ is **Results - Measuring Results & Sustaining Momentum.** Without this rhythm of reflection, recognition, and recalibration, even the strongest foundation will eventually stall. It's not about obsessing over every metric; rather, it's about creating rituals that help you see your own evolution. The idea is that you can keep building, even when it's hard to tell if the bricks are stacking up.

Why Most People and Businesses Lose Momentum

Starting is easy. Anyone can start anything. Staying consistent is where most fall apart. One of the key contributors to keeping that momentum is tracking your progress. When you don't track your progress, you feel like you aren't making any, and that can feel defeating. When you don't celebrate your wins, you lose your motivation. When you don't adapt your strategy, you plateau, no matter how hard you're working. As a result, even though you are moving forward, or on the edge of a breakthrough, you end up feeling stuck, discouraged, and you stop. You can't see it. Implementing ways to measure this progress, celebrate the wins, and build solid strategy is one of the crucial keys to scaling up.

"People who track small, daily progress are more than twice as likely to stay motivated long-term."
– Harvard Business Review, The Progress Principle

The Power of Small Wins and Seeing Your Own Growth

There was a stretch of time when I started to feel hollow inside. Almost like I was on auto pilot. I was doing all the things I was supposed to. Working long hours, hitting deadlines, and showing up every day. From the outside, everything looked fine-steady, successful. And it was. But inside, I felt like I was walking through quicksand. Every day was a repeat of the last. Maybe I was moving, but I couldn't feel the movement. I had no idea. There was no sense of going forward.

This made me feel stuck, and I started to have doubts about what I was doing. Was it right? Did it really matter at all? In Bosnia, we have this saying: "boil the water, cool the water" — it essentially means you are constantly heating up the water and then cooling it. So you are someone who is constantly very busy…it's just that you aren't really making any progress. I felt like that. I had all these obligations and contracts in place. Pulling out and switching directions wasn't an easy task. Regardless, I started to wonder if I was wasting my time. Was all this effort was adding up to anything at all? I wasn't seeing big breakthroughs. I wasn't having any lightning bolt moments. Just slow, silent days. And that silence began to gnaw at me.

One afternoon, my ADHD kicked in, and I decided to break up this mundane day with by moving some things around my closet. Another task that felt like "boiling the water, cooling the water", but it was really an attempt to quiet the noise in my mind. It was then that I found it! My old journal, wedged in a corner of a box I hadn't touched in years. When I was evacuated for medical treatment I left without my parents, and the way I felt connected to them was by writing in this journal. Telling them everything I did, my goals, my plans. It was written as though I was talking to them. I clearly described my challenges, not only medically, but also cultural shocks and my adjustment to living in the U.S.. I was just a kid trying to piece together some semblance of a life through sitcoms I watched, and working hard on learning English.

That day in my closet, I opened the journal more out of habit more than curiosity, because I already knew what was in it. But then I started to read. And I froze.

The handwriting was mine, but it felt like I was reading someone else's life. The person on those pages didn't speak any English and was describing how an 80+ year old Holocaust survivor, Renata, was teaching her English and the goal was to write one paragraph about the moon. The more I read, the more I saw that her fears were loud - everything was so new and different, like putting ice in soup, and just in general using so much ice in everything. That girl was unsure how to navigate American culture, and overwhelmed by the weight of trauma she hadn't yet named. And the person on these pages had dreams, but they were simple, desperate dreams. To survive, feel safe, and just be normal.

Like a ton of bricks, it hit me. Here I was, sitting years later, running my own company with Fortune 100 clients. Fluent in a language I had once stumbled through. Coaching executives, and creating cutting edge software. Speaking on stages, leading teams. Building a life that the little girl in that journal couldn't have even imagined.

This realization took my breath away. For the first time in a long time, I saw myself clearly. I saw how far I had moved. I could see in front of me where I started and where I was now. The fear that once kept me silent was gone. The weight that once crushed me had lifted. I had become someone I didn't even know I was becoming. And the only reason I hadn't noticed was because I wasn't tracking it.

In almost an instant, my restless feelings left and now I wondered - *what else had I missed in all of my work as a result of not measuring it? What progress have I made without noticing it?* I felt like I had to go back and review, like I should have celebrated all of those wins. Those wins were owed to me after lots of hard work, after all.

From that day on, I made a new commitment: to measure what matters. Not just the big wins, but even the invisible ones. The mindset shifts. The moments of courage. The days I showed up when it would've been easier not to.

Because when you track your growth, you start to believe in it again. And when you believe in your growth, you keep going. You become your own cheerleader, your own motivation, and your own inspiration. You keep encouraging yourself to keep moving forward.

We all know that simple pleasure of checking the box after item on our to-do list has been completed. It's such a simple thing, but we all love it. It's because each time we do this, a little burst of good hormones enter our body. Heck, sometimes I write things into my list just so I can check them off. I learned this lesson a hard way. I missed so many moments that I should have celebrated and now, I don't miss any. You don't need anyone for this. You can do it yourself, because you know. No matter how small or how invisible - if you have moved on and completed it — give yourself a big pat on the back. You deserve it. As you get into habit of doing this, measuring results will be fun and almost addictive.

This isn't just about personal growth; it's the foundation of business growth too.

Take Peloton, for example. On the surface, it's a fitness company. But behind the sleek bikes and charismatic instructors is a powerful system designed to turn invisible progress into visible momentum. Stationary bikes have existed for almost a couple centuries, and they became really popular in the 1980s with the rise of the fitness industry. But Peloton made stationary bikes, a potentially boring activity, almost addicting. Their brand is not built on performance alone. It is built it on perception—on helping people see their own growth, day by day, ride by ride.

From your very first workout, the platform begins tracking everything: your output, your cadence, your heart rate, your personal records. But that's not just useless data, it's feedback for the rider. It's a mirror held up to your own effort. And besides being a mirror that reflects back your effort, it further celebrates that effort with you. Whether it's a virtual high five, a shoutout from an instructor when you hit a milestone, or a badge that appears when you complete a streak, Peloton turns progress into something you feel. You want to show up again and again. People stay consistent because they feel like what they are doing is working. Peloton gives them that feeling, over and over again, by measuring what matters and celebrating it out loud.

"Peloton didn't just build a fitness brand—they built a momentum engine. By tracking personal records, celebrating streaks, and turning progress into emotion, they kept people coming back—not out of discipline, but belief."

And that's what great businesses do. They create feedback loops that fuel momentum. They make it easy for people to see that they're improving, even when the big transformation hasn't happened yet. In doing so, they don't just drive results, they sustain them.

The 3 Momentum Shifts That Keep You Scaling Up

1. The "Measure What Matters" Shift

Track Progress to Keep Growing

You can't systematically improve what you don't measure-it's as simple as that. But more importantly, you can't trust your growth unless you've seen it with your own eyes. So it's almost counterintuitive, but the real reason most people avoid measuring is it can be scary. What if the results and numbers don't match the effort exerted? The truth might hurt more than the guesswork and limbo. Unfortunately, what happens if you won't measure is that you rob yourself of the proof that you are making any progress - which is far worse than the possible need to pivot and course correct. Without that proof, motivation starts to quietly die or you work on the wrong things. That's why this shift is so powerful. It gives you your power back. Power to see what is happening and if you need to pivot, as well as, most importantly, celebrate the progress you did make.

When you start measuring and creating specific goals, you stop chasing vague success and start focusing on meaningful progress and momentum. Please note that you don't want to measure some vanity metrics or stats just to check off this box. You need to find three to five numbers that truly reflect your goal. Maybe it's revenue, or client retention, skills learned, or the number of focused work blocks completed. It can be anything, but what matters is that the numbers align with your values, reflect your goals, and that you track them with honesty.

This approach isn't just feel-good. It's backed by research. A study from Harvard Business Review found that people who tracked small, daily progress in meaningful work were twice as likely to stay motivated and engaged long-term, even when external results were slow to arrive. They called it the "Progress Principle." Because even minor wins, when visible, create major momentum.

"You might not see your progress day to day—but one day, you'll look back and realize you became everything you once prayed for."

One great example of this comes from software company Atlassian, makers of tools like Jira and Trello. Rather than obsess over traditional metrics like top-line revenue, at Atlassian they believed that happy, productive teams build better products. So they famously focused on tracking developer satisfaction and time-to-solve metrics. That shift in measurement helped them become one of the fastest-growing enterprise software companies in the world.

So ask yourself: What actually moves the needle in your business or your life? What behaviors, when done consistently, generate results over time? What signals tell you that you're in alignment? And then, start tracking those. Review them with courage. Pivot if you have to.

That's how you stop spinning your wheels and start growing with purpose and clear direction.

2. The "Celebrate Wins" Shift

Recognize Progress to Stay Energized

Most people move the goalpost so fast, they forget to honor the moment they just crossed the last one. It's like we are trained not to slow down because we have to chase the next big thing. And if you are on the right path, absolutely, chase it. But before you do, take a pause to celebrate your progress. Because without that pause, without that breath of acknowledgment, the journey starts to feel hollow and heavy.

This is one of the most overlooked reasons people lose motivation. It's not because they're tired (resting will help if you are tired). It's because they've become emotionally disconnected from their own progress. It's execution on autopilot. They're chasing growth, but never stopping long enough to feel it. And when that happens, even massive achievements can feel like…nothing. Empty.

Celebration isn't fluff. It's fuel for your body and soul. It's the nervous system signal that says, "This matters. Do more of this." It's the fire that keeps you going.

When we celebrate progress, no matter how small, we reinforce all behaviors that got us there. We recognize all of the previous building blocks, even if they aren't named as such. We activate a reward loop that helps us stay consistent. This isn't just theory. A study published in the Journal of Personality and Social Psychology found that individuals who celebrated small victories were significantly more likely to stick to long-term goals than those who didn't. The act of celebrating, even something as simple as a moment of reflection or a high-five, increases dopamine levels and deepens motivation.

In business, this principle is used by some of the most successful organizations in the world. At Zappos, celebration is embedded into the company culture. When a customer support team member receives positive feedback, it's shared publicly. There are "rockstar" shoutouts, bell rings for big wins, and even impromptu parades around the office. They know that recognizing effort breeds great energy, and that great energy sustains excellence.

And the same is true for you.

Whether you're leading a team, running a business, or navigating a personal transformation, you need to build moments of recognition into your rhythm. It could be a quarterly celebration of progress, or a simple reflection journal at the end of each week. It could be a message of gratitude to your team, or even just a silent nod to yourself in the mirror—"You did that." It doesn't matter how small it might be, as long as it is authentic and celebrated. Remember that this journey you are on, the journey of scaling up, isn't just about scaling the numbers. It's scaling your joy, your fulfillment, and, most of all, it's about scaling you as a whole. Scaling your feeling of being alive and aligned with your purpose. The more you honor that feeling and recognize it, the more of it you'll create.

3. The "Next Level" Shift

Set New Targets to Keep Momentum Alive

The entire point of this book is leading to this shift right here — the "Next Level" Shift. This is also the number one reason you need to measure the results, because this shift keeps you scaling up, over and over again.

One of the most dangerous places to stagnate and fall behind is that moment right after a big win. The moment when you cross the finish line, and hit that goal. You take a breath, and everything feels completed. Oh, it's a wonderful feeling. I know it well, and I love it. It's my preferred way of reaching an internal high. But if you are not careful, something subtle starts to happen. Almost unnoticed. Urgency stops, clarity fades, and the things that propelled you forward dissolve into stillness because you don't have to do them any more.

Because it's a planned completion, that feels good and not like a failure. You relax and start to coast. That becomes even more dangerous because coasting feels safe. Years go by, the celebration and big win you had are now in the past, and you get lost without even realizing it. All this because you stopped asking "What's next"?

Success, if not followed by vision, creates a quiet kind of stagnation. A lull that looks like rest but slowly erodes momentum.

I am not saying don't celebrate and enjoy your wins, or take the time to rest, regroup, and enjoy the quiet. Absolutely do so. But also start thinking and defining your next target. Your next goal. Your next level. Those who keep scaling up aren't just setting goals, they are stacking goals as well. They are continually scaling up and becoming the best version of themselves. In the process, they are creating the best organizations and leading teams.

To keep your scaling momentum alive, you have to recognize the moment when healthy rest begins to slip into a comfort zone that holds you back—and know when it's time to pull yourself out, look up, and scan the horizon for your next goal. But not just any goal. The right next level. The kind that stretches you to the edge of inspiration. You need to find that "Goldilocks Zone." This term refers to goals that are not too easy and not too hard, but just challenging enough to activate excitement without triggering overwhelm.

In one study published in Psychological Review, researchers found that individuals who consistently pursued slightly beyond-current-capacity goals maintained higher long-term motivation than those who chose "realistic" or "safe" targets. You've probably seen this in action. Think of how Apple doesn't just release new products, they redefine categories. How Patagonia doesn't just sell clothing, they scale environmental impact with each new line. These aren't just businesses hitting goals. They're expanding the frame of what's possible. And you can do the same.

So ask yourself:

- What would it look like to stretch just 10% beyond where you are right now?
- What's a version of you—or your company—that scares you a little, but excites you even more?
- What next-level vision would require a slightly bolder version of you to step forward?

This isn't about endless striving. It's about continuous unfolding. It's a way of meeting the world, with your eyes open, your energy forward, and your heart still hungry for what's next.

A Challenge to Start Now

It's not enough to understand momentum. For momentum to make a difference, you actually have to build it. You have to do the work. So why not start now? Track it. Honor it. Stretch it.

So here's your challenge:

Pick one key metric. Just one. Something you'll track, daily or weekly, for the next 30 days. It doesn't have to be big or impressive. In fact, the smaller and more meaningful, the better. Maybe it's the number of focused hours you work. Maybe it's your water intake, your sleep quality, or the number of follow-up emails you send. Maybe it's client testimonials, dollars saved, or minutes spent in creative flow.

Whatever it is, make it matter to you. Make it something that reflects the future you're building. And then start tracking it. Not with pressure, but with presence. Celebrate every movement. See how it feels, and let the data show you what your brain forgets: that you are evolving.

And if you're bold enough, share it on socials. Post it publicly. Tell a friend. Create a streak chart and stick it on your wall. Because accountability is about witnessing. Because the most powerful form of leadership is leading by example. Because leaders turn private growth into turning shared momentum. That's how leaders rise. That's how movements begin. And that's how you take the invisible and make it real.

Scaling Isn't About Reaching the End—It's About Building Forever

Scaling is not a one-time achievement. It's a way of living, working, leading, and thinking. It's how you live. How you lead. How you meet every next chapter of your life, with curiosity, with courage, and with the quiet belief that more is always possible.

The moment you stop measuring, you lose your compass. The moment you stop celebrating, you lose your joy. The moment you stop stretching, you stop growing. But when you build these rhythms into your life you create a cycle of momentum that compounds. So keep tracking. Keep celebrating. Keep reaching. The next level isn't your finish line, it's your foundation.

And in the next—and final—chapter, we'll bring it all together. We'll solidify your Scale Up Blueprint™ and lay the groundwork for a legacy built not just on success... but on continuous, unstoppable growth. Let's finish strong. You've come this far. Now let's go even farther.

Checklist

Building Block - 7 Results

Measuring Results & Sustaining Momentum

Quick Win Checklist:

- ✓ Identify your top three success metrics for the next 90 days.
- ✓ Create a simple tracking system (spreadsheet, journal, or app) and log your progress weekly.
- ✓ Schedule a monthly "review and refine" session to adjust your actions.
- ✓ Choose one ritual to celebrate progress — no matter how small the win.
- ✓ Identify one next-level goal you'll work toward once your current target is achieved.

Shareable Content:

Your Turn:

Pick one small thing that matters, and start tracking it. Not to control, but to witness yourself. For the next 30 days, commit to just one metric:

- Hours in flow
- Sales made
- Workouts completed
- Kind words spoken
- Sleep quality
- Water intake
- Pages written
- Or something else uniquely yours.

Track it. Celebrate it. Let it show you what your memory might forget: You're evolving. You're moving. You're already rising.

Share your progress publicly. Use the hashtag #ScaleUpBlueprint to join a movement of leaders committed to building momentum that lasts.

Social Media Ready:

Stop measuring success by what's visible. Start measuring it by what's compounding. Energy. Alignment. Joy. Those are metrics that matter. #ScaleUpBlueprint

The next level isn't a finish line. It's a new foundation. Build it by measuring, celebrating, and reaching again. That's the rhythm of sustainable growth. #ScaleUpBlueprint

Most people don't burn out from working too hard. They burn out because they can't see their own progress. Track what matters. Celebrate every step. That's how momentum is built. #ScaleUpBlueprint

You don't need a full strategy. You need a *streak*. One tiny action. Repeated daily. Celebrated intentionally. That's how transformation begins. #ScaleUpBlueprint

Your Legacy

The Scale Up Mindset – A Blueprint for Life and Leadership

Success isn't a finish line. It's a way of life. Success isn't about checking off goals so you can finally coast. It's about building a mindset, a structure, and a rhythm that allows you to rise, scale, and lead, over and over again.

By now, you've walked through every part of the Scale Up Blueprint™. You've seen how each building block connects to the next, how they reinforce one another, and how together they create an unshakable foundation for exponential growth.

But the real magic doesn't happen just by reading. It happens when you live the Scale Up Blueprint. Growth is not a one-time experience, it's a daily decision. And the moment you embrace that, not just intellectually but fully and deeply, you begin to live differently. You stop looking for the moment you "arrive," and you start living in the momentum you've built.

I believe that we are all infinite beings and that any person can scale to any heights they desire to, using this Scale Up blue print.

The Moment I Realized Scaling Is a Way of Life

For years, my life was built around massive goals: Survive. Walk. Drive. Graduate. Start a business. Own a home. Live on the beach. I worked relentlessly. I checked every box. One day, I looked around and realized... I had made it. I had reached the life I once thought I would never have. But instead of feeling complete, I felt in my gut that this wasn't the end. That this was the beginning of something even greater. I didn't know what, I just knew.

What I learned since is that the real win weren't the beach house, the business, or any of my milestones. The real win is the person I had become along the way. The strength that I have built. The character I had shaped. Resilience I earned. Expanding beyond anything I could have possibly imagined.

That is when I understood that scaling isn't about achieving, it's about becoming. Becoming the best version of yourself. It's about pushing into discomfort to grow into the best and the most evolved version of yourself. It's about setting new goals because you know you're capable of more. It's about teaching, measuring, and celebrating.

That's why I chose to share this message, and why I became a speaker. It wasn't just to help others grow and justify my existence and survival. It was because this work continues to stretch me. It pushes me to rise to new levels, to lead, and never stop building. Because one day, when my life comes to an end, I want to look back and say:

"Wow. That was an amazing ride. I didn't just survive. I lived. I grew. I scaled. I gave it everything I had."

And I want the same thing for you.

Final Thought: The Legacy You Leave Behind

This may be a cliche but it has to be said because I feel the need to remind you of the words you may have already heard. At the end of your life, no one will ask how many hours you worked, and how you never took a vacation. They won't list your job titles. They won't quote your resume.

But they will remember how you showed up. They'll remember your courage. Your kindness. Your leadership. Your presence. In your work and your personal life. They'll remember the way you made them feel. The way you made them believe in more. The way you inspired them to rise.

That's legacy.

And you get to shape that legacy, starting now. So don't wait.

This is your moment. This is your time to Scale Up.

With you on the journey,

Maja

"You were never meant to stay the same. You were built to evolve, to expand, to rise—and in doing so, leave behind a legacy of growth, courage, and possibility, to create a life that echoes."

— *Maja Kazazic*

Ready to Go Deeper?

You don't have to do this alone, or guess your way through growth. To help you implement the Scale Up Blueprint™ in your real life, I've created two powerful (and free) resources:

The Scale Up Action Workbook — Your guided space to reflect, plan, and take aligned action

www.MajaKazazic.com/ScaleUpWorkbook

The Scale Up Quiz — Discover which building block you're strongest in, and where your next breakthrough might be waiting.

www.MajaKazazic.com/ScaleUpQuiz

These tools are designed to meet you exactly where you are, and help you keep building, one intentional step at a time.

 Scan for the companion workbook, discussion guide, and bonus tools.

Bring the ScaleUp Blueprint to your team or event.
Visit: www.MajaKazazic.com/ScaleUp

Resources

You've learned the 7 Building Blocks. Now let's build your next level—together.

Reader Hub & Tools
Download the companion workbook, discussion guide, and printable frameworks: MajaKazazic.com/ScaleUp

Quiz: Find Your Scale Up Archetype
Discover your current growth pattern and next best move; results map to the Building Blocks: MajaKazazic.com/ScaleUp

Speaking & Workshops
For keynotes, leadership workshops, or team trainings based on the Scale Up Blueprint™, visit MajaKazazic.com/ScaleUp.

Bulk & Corporate Orders
For discounted bulk purchases and custom bundles (books + workshop/Q&A), inquire via the contact form at MajaKazazic.com/ScaleUp.

Stay Connected
Share your takeaways with the hashtag #ScaleUpBlueprint and tag me so I can cheer you on.

This isn't about doing more. It's about scaling smarter—with structure, with soul, and with support.

Acknowledgments

There are far too many people to name here who have shaped this book and the person behind it. If you shared a story, made an introduction, offered feedback, or simply stood beside me when the ground felt unsteady, you are in these pages.

One name, though, must be written out loud: **Rosie**—my dog, a Great Dane, and my quiet teacher. You reminded me every day that love can be both fierce and gentle. Thank you for carrying me through the hardest years, one soft nudge at a time.

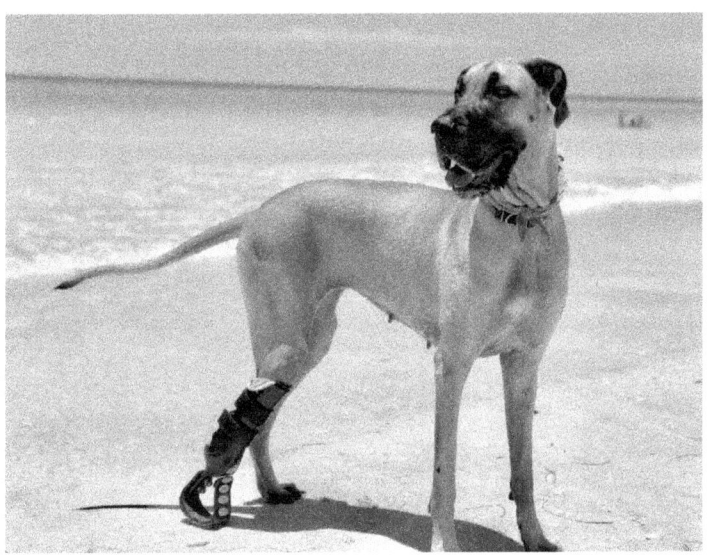

About the Author

Maja Kazazic is a resilience expert, keynote speaker, and entrepreneur who scaled from war-zone survivor to business leader. After surviving a grenade attack during the Bosnian genocide, she immigrated to the United States and rebuilt her life from the ground up. She founded a successful IT company and has spent two decades helping leaders and teams—from startups to Fortune 100—scale with clarity and momentum.

Blending lived adversity with in-the-trenches business experience, Maja teaches growth, grit, and disciplined execution. The Scale Up Blueprint captures her seven Building Blocks that leaders can stack to create durable results.

For keynotes, workshops, and resources, visit MajaKazazic.com/ScaleUp.

Index

A

accountability; see also measurement; momentum 146, 176

adaptability; change readiness; decision speed 6, 11, 15, 18, 25, 31, 40, 51, 55, 60, 83, 107, 120, 125, 132, 133, 134, 136, 142, 144, 152, 160, 180

adversity; reframing; micro-wins 38, 51, 89, 186

archetypes, Scale Up; diagnostic use 21

B

bias for action; starting small; compounding 41

boundaries; energy management; saying no 7

building blocks, the seven; overview 37

C

cadence; operating rhythm; weekly reviews 169

change, leading through; communication 7, 16, 31, 39, 40, 44, 69, 81, 94, 113, 120, 121, 124, 136, 137, 144

clarity; decision filters; north star 2, 9, 44, 46, 70, 76, 125, 134, 142, 174, 186

coachability; feedback loops 44, 170

D

decision frameworks; trade-offs; risk 184

discipline & consistency (Block #5) 132

discipline; habit stacking; consistency 35

E

emotional regulation; leadership presence 44, 61, 65, 68, 69, 97, 153

energy management; recovery; self-care 117

esilience; recovery; post-setback plans 36, 42, 43, 47, 94, 148, 153, 181

execution; prioritization; focus sprints 2, 41, 43, 172, 186

F

feedback; loops; retrospectives 44

flywheel; momentum; compoundi 45

G

goals; leading indicators; trailing indicators 5, 14, 17, 21, 22, 27-31, 33, 42, 44, 75, 80, 83, 93, 115, 123, 124, 135, 137, 140, 141, 167, 171, 173, 175, 180, 181

grit; setbacks; resilience practices 36, 42, 43, 49, 149, 152, 186

H

habits; systems; environment design 37, 40, 42, 44, 116, 119, 129, 136

I

influence; credibility; trust 35, 68, 69, 116

iterations; pilots; experiments 139

K

keynotes; storytelling; application to business 184, 186

L

leadership; self-leadership; team alignment 1

leverage, strategic; networks; mentors 9, 123

leveraging support & strategic networks (Block #1) 49

M

measurement; dashboards; review cadence 44, 172

measuring results & sustaining momentum (Block #7) 165

momentum; micro-wins; streaks 1, 2, 8, 9, 11, 13, 32, 36, 40, 41, 43, 44, 60, 109, 113, 117, 119, 121, 123, 128, 129, 131, 136, 140, 143, 144, 145, 157, 158, 161, 162, 164, 166, 169-171, 174-177, 179, 180, 186

N

narrative, personal; origin story; meaning-making 1, 5, 14, 18, 51, 52, 69, 84, 118, 119, 133, 137, 140, 142, 160, 161, 169, 170, 173, 182

networks; support systems; peer councils 38, 59, 66, 73

O

operating system; weekly/monthly rhythms 8

ownership; radical responsibility 63, 66

P

prioritization; saying no; focus 132

purpose; values; vision ii, 3, 4, 8, 9, 14, 31, 46, 67, 96, 108, 139, 172, 174

R

reviews, weekly/monthly/quarterly 176, 178

S

self-care; sustainable growth 139

setbacks; bounce-back; reframes 148, 152, 163

support, leveraging; asking for help 8, 35-38, 41, 48, 50-52, 56- 67, 70-76, 80, 92, 93, 102, 103, 107, 118, 119, 124, 132, 133, 135, 153, 160, 173, 184

systems; workflows; SOPs 2, 8, 26, 41, 42, 44, 52, 59, 60, 67, 71-73, 76, 86, 123, 124, 129, 134, 144, 147, 160

T

tenacity; long games; antifragility 36, 43, 144, 149, 152-157, 159, 160, 164

tenacity & overcoming setbacks (Block #6) 148

trust; psychological safety 1, 30, 36, 63, 65, 66, 69, 71, 103, 105, 106, 116, 120, 124, 125, 142, 170

U

unlocking hidden potential (Block #3) 92

V

vision; constraints; opportunity finding 8, 35, 49, 59, 61, 63, 66, 69, 70, 72, 76, 87, 126, 132, 133, 134, 137, 144, 152, 174, 175

W

weekly scorecards; KPIs 176

workbooks & tools; companion resources ii, 1, 5, 6, 7, 13, 16, 30, 33, 39-42, 45, 47, 50, 59, 62, 81, 82, 84, 85, 87, 90, 101, 107, 111, 114, 116, 119, 121-122, 126-127, 132-135, 137-140, 146, 151, 156-160, 164, 168, 171, 176, 178, 181, 182

www.ingramcontent.com/pod-product-compliance
Lightning Source LLC
Chambersburg PA
CBHW040233110526
44582CB00002B/41